TELL IT
TO THE
CHURCH

TELL IT TO THE CHURCH

LYNN R. BUZZARD
&
LAURENCE ECK

Tyndale House Publishers, Inc.
WHEATON, ILLINOIS

First printing, Tyndale House edition, July 1985

Library of Congress Catalog Card Number 85-80046
ISBN 0-8423-6986-4

In appreciation to Michael Weeks, who first challenged the Christian Legal Society with this ministry of reconciliation, to C. Fred Cassity, who pursued it to fruition, and to our wives, Juanita Buzzard and Pam Eck, who have always embodied it.

CONTENTS

A Brawling Bride

The wedding guests have gathered in great anticipation; the ceremony to be performed today has long been awaited. The orchestra begins to play an anthem, and the choir rises in proper precision. The bridegroom and his attendants gather in front of the chancel. One little saint, her flowered hat bobbing, leans to her companion and whispers, "Isn't he handsome?" The response is agreement, "My, yes. The handsomest. . . ."

The sound of the organ rises, a joyous announcement that the bride is coming. Everyone stands and strains to get a proper glimpse of the beauty. Then a horrible gasp explodes from the congregation. This is a bride like no other.

In she stumbles. Something terrible has happened! One leg is twisted; she limps pronouncedly. The wedding garment is tattered and muddy; great rents in her dress leave her scarcely modest. Black bruises can be seen welting her bare arms; the bride's nose is bloody. An eye is swollen, yellow and purple in its discoloration. Patches of hair look as if they had actually been pulled from her scalp.

▶9

Fumbling over the keys, the organist begins again after his shocked pause. The attendants cast their eyes down. The congregation mourns silently. Surely the Bridegroom deserved better than this! That handsome Prince who has kept himself faithful to his love should find consummation with the most beautiful of women—not this. His bride, the church, has been fighting again.[1]

PART 1 THE DILEMMA

1

WHEN IN DOUBT, SUE!

News of bizarre lawsuits is common today. A woman in Texas brought suit against a veterinarian for negligently shearing curls from her pet Afghan. She sought and won damages of $468.00. The doctor arrived with the money in pennies, and began to count it out penny by penny, whereupon the woman's attorney called in the news media. When the press appeared, the doctor threatened a further suit for libel. This case took three years and three sets of lawyers.

Gail Dickie, a gymnast, filed suit against the *Guinness Book of World Records* and ABC for $5 million for failing to list her record of 13,104 sit-ups in a contest in California. That is $381.56 per sit-up.

Suing is news. It is even entertainment. "Court calendars are clogged with cupidity," declared one observer. But this is far from funny. Call it rather a national tragedy. The movie *Kramer vs. Kramer* pictured the brutality. Ted's lawyer tells him, "Ted, this is a dirty game we're in. . . . So think dirty." And at the end of the movie Ted cries out to Joanna, "The things we've done to each other."

When Lee Marvin was asked what he'd

learned after the lawsuit in which his live-in lover sued him for "palimony," he said, "How to lie. . . . Everyone lied." And it is infectious. Lawsuits breed further suits, countersuits, claims against other parties. Lawsuits breed suspicion, defensiveness, anger, and bitterness.

A recent book *Sue the Bastards!* begins with this ominous statement: "The purpose of this book is to make you armed and dangerous." The book then proceeds to suggest ways in which you can "get even" by suing neighbors, companies, stores, manufacturers, landlords, and auto dealers. The title reflects a mood that focuses on "rights" and assertiveness.

So extensive is litigation in our society that Marlene Adler Marks declared in *The Suing of America:* "Suing has become an American parlor game. Obsession with suing is part of the American character." And Roger Simon, writing in the *Chicago Sun Times,* noted ". . . whenever an American feels embarrassed and heartsick, he is sure to sue somebody."

The statistics bear this out: 22,000 lawsuits are filed every day! Twenty times as many lawyers (per capita) practice in the United States as in Japan. In terms of civil complaints, many European nations have about 300-400 suits per 100,000 population; this can be compared to 5,000 suits per 100,000 population in the United States. And that does not include the disputes that are never taken to a lawyer, or those taken to counsel but where no complaint is filed. One out of every two Americans will sue someone, sometime.

The rush to the courts to solve both personal and corporate conflicts is so overwhelming that judicial authorities are pleading for alternatives—methods that are cheaper, faster, and more humane. A head-line in the June 8, 1981 issue of the *National Law Journal* proclaimed: "Got a spat? Go Rent a Judge." The article described the "rebirth of private justice," whereby parties select a person outside the courts to serve as a judge. "It's one of those things whose time has come," declared Oregon Supreme Court administrator David Gernant.

WHY ARE WE SO ANGRY?

Why has suing become an American way of life? Part of the reason rests in the destructive character of certain aspects of our life-style. Gone are many of the primary social structures (extended family, neighborhood groups, social organizations), which in an earlier generation absorbed much of the interpersonal conflict that now ends up in court. Persons are far more likely to call the police complaining about an errant dog or child than go to a neighbor even a few doors away.

The sense of community these social institutions engendered has faded. We have resorted to the formalized institutions and structures of the law to "right" the wrong, to protest, to seek compensation, to demand justice. Our radical individualism fosters the loss of common identity and turns those who get in our way into things—enemies, opponents, defendants. Since I don't belong to you, nor you to me, I can attack you. Strikingly, 80 percent of civil cases involve parties who are not strangers, people with some relationship beyond the dispute: employer-employee, business associates, neighbors, family members.

Another contributing factor is that we are in the midst of a generation tutored on "rights." Know your rights. Get your rights. Assert them; assure them. We are told to

▶15

watch out for people who take advantage of us or deny us one of our rights. If we do not assert ourselves, we are supposed to be weak and unfulfilled. Our society says: "If a man takes your coat, sue him for everything he's got!"

Robert J. Ringer's book *Looking Out for Number One* warns against being intimidated by other people's counsel about what is right. "Forget the 'moral' standards others may have tried to cram down your throat. . . ." Especially, he says, watch out for the "moralist. And above all, don't swim in the dangerous and uncivilized waters of self-sacrifice."

Next add the good old American sense of fighting and winning to this increased focus on individualism and loss of community. We are, after all, a nation of the Yankees, IBM, and Coca-Cola. A nation of firsts. Our sports, to quote one supposed authority, mirror our culture: "Winning is" after all, "not the most important thing. It is the only thing." Life is a game, and winning is everything. Indeed the fight itself becomes a thrill.

Douglas Matthews *(Sue the Bastards!)* catches the spirit of this when he describes what can happen to the litigator: "If you do sue and are lucky, you are going to get to the point in your adventures when a wave of joyful calm engulfs your feelings on the case at point, where the specific facts involved no longer matter, where the money no longer matters, where as a fact, nothing seems to matter much any longer except the sweet nectar of seeing your right vindicated. You will have surpassed spite and achieved existential fury."

The need for individuals to be right is so great, observes Reuel Howe, that "they are willing to sacrifice themselves, their relationships, and even love, for it."

Add to these dimensions the materialism of our society and you have all the ingredients of a litigious, suing society. Materialism so shapes our thinking of justice that dollar values are given to our complaints. Consider the $850,000 award to Virginia O'Hare against a doctor for a negligent tummy tuck that resulted in a navel two inches off center. Or what of Thomas Harris's (author of *I'm OK, You're OK)* suit for $19 million against a pastor from Ohio for mistakenly indicating in a radio sermon that Harris had committed suicide.

People are hurt and they want dollars. People are angry and they want dollars. People are injured and they want dollars.

This hurt and insecurity create an almost instinctive reaction of blame and hostility that leads to the filing of a lawsuit. It's instinctive. To the Christian, J. B. Phillip's translation of Romans 8:13 should be instructive. "If . . . you cut the nerve of your instinctive action by obeying the Spirit, you are on your way to real living." Christians are called to live by far different standards than our battle-oriented society.

And yet churches have found themselves entangled in legal battles against other churches, against businesses, and in disputes within their own local or denominational bodies. In a Colorado city, a lawsuit was filed seeking to oust a pastor from the church. New locks were placed on church doors.

Two prominent foreign missions groups sued each other recently over libel, each alleging a whole series of "wrongs" against the other. An Arizona church recently spent virtually all its resources seeking to vindicate its name in a lawsuit with a local paper and a former church member. Several very prominent Christian musicians and composers have brought suit against thirty Christian radio stations. And this is only a representative list!

As Christians we have not applied the Scriptures to our own institutional or individual lives. Jesus' commandment to love one another has been nullified by division, litigation, and hostility. At times a veritable civil war has been fought out in the Christian community. One is reminded of the story of Stonewall Jackson's observation of fighting among his own men. He reportedly told them: "Remember, gentlemen, the enemy is over there."

But an alternative does exist. News of a different kind of legal conflict was carried on the front page of the *Los Angeles Times* on April 11, 1980. The article was titled "Legal Fights End Up in Church Halls." It told of a radically different approach to legal conflict initiated by the Christian Conciliation Service of the Christian Legal Society—a process that seeks to avoid the adversarial, "fight-it-out" style of litigation. This process is built on a belief that disputes between Christians belong in the church, not in court.

Russell Chandler, the *Times* religion editor, described the scene he saw:

The two attorneys walked into the room and sat down opposite each other. So did the parents and stepparents of a 10-year-old boy, who, that recent morning, was the center of attention. Both couples wanted custody of the youngster.

This could have been the scene of a bitter court battle, just one of millions of disputes that clog the nation's judicial system each year.

But, from the outset, something was different about this case.

As he introduced the proceeding, Los Angeles lawyer C. Fred Cassity turned to the couples and the boy and said, "As we hear one another today, if we are eloquent and persuasive and do everything right procedurally, but fail to exhibit true love, one for another, the process has failed. This issue today is not 'winning' but determining God's will in this specific case. . . .

"It is primarily this quality that sets these proceedings apart from anything the world can offer."

The custody case was "tried," not in court, but in a church.

The decision was made, not by a judge, but by five church elders.

And instead of charging fees, the attorneys donated their services. Each couple gave a nominal gift to their church.

Christian doctrines and convictions are almost custom-made for conflict resolution and healing: the doctrine of reconciliation, the doctrine of forgiveness, and the doctrine of the covenant and its application in restoring broken relationships. The church is the gifted and equipped body of Christ.

Of all the doctrines of the church, perhaps none is more applicable than the gifts of the Holy Spirit: patience and long-suffering, wisdom and discernment, healing, peacemaking. Christ, the Reconciler, did not grasp after rights and privileges, he gave them up (Phil. 2:5-11). He recognized, but conquered, the divisive and debilitating powers of evil, sin, and death. His life modeled giving, not defending. His teaching emphasized releasing, not protecting. And his death demonstrated participatory love, not abstract justice.

How effective the church would be in our day if it could become a great healer in the legal arena—a great restorer of relationships, peace, and harmony. Imagine the powerful witness of reconciled Jews and gentiles in the first century. Here were hostile people, who had been separated and alienated, now praying, rejoicing, and ministering together. Perhaps the declaration of Christ's reconciliation was easier to believe because the world saw it manifested in the believing community's relationships.

The church surely has the calling, the church has the concepts, the church has the gifts, and the church has the Lord. All that remains is for the church to have the will to hear the call of Scripture for the reconciled to be agents of reconciliation.

In this book we will show how the church can assume such a ministry of reconciliation. But first we must look at the crisis in our current legal system and the inherent conflict that exists within our society. Both of these dimensions are part of the dilemma that we face as Christians living in the twentieth century.

2 CRISIS AT THE BAR

Harold Berman, the noted Harvard law professor, writes in *The Interaction of Law and Religion* that western man is undergoing an integrity crisis. "Our whole culture seems to be facing the possibility of a nervous breakdown. . . . One major symptom of this threatened breakdown is the massive loss of confidence in the law. . . ."

Of course, criticism of law and lawyers is nothing new. It was Dicke Butcher in Shakespeare's play *Henry VI* who suggested that the first thing to do was to "kill all the lawyers." They were conspicuously absent in Thomas More's *Utopia*. The Talmud refers to them as "oppressors and robbers," and Plato thought they were "small, unrighteous souls." The critique today of law goes far beyond these expressions of individual frustration.

So extensive are the doubts about our legal system, both by those within and without, that it amounts to what one author called a "crisis at the bar." John P. Frank, in *American Law: The Case for Radical Reform*, foresaw the same collapse as Berman: "We are approaching the total bankruptcy of our remedy system . . . and we are making no effort to escape a legal doomsday." Frank went on to compare people today to people in the crowd surrounding Samson in the Philistine temple who were "unaware of the impending surprise and headache."

Particularly relevant is the widespread recognition that the legal system fails to meet the needs of many of our citizens. Seven million poor have legal problems every year, not including criminal charges, yet, as President Carter said, "Ninety percent of our lawyers serve 10 percent of our people."

Many are concerned that all too often court decisions only indirectly relate to justice. So profound is this crisis at the bar that Judge Lois Forer titled her volume *The Death of the Law* and writes of a "mindless, archaic system, which produces results that have little to do with justice."

Indeed the legal profession has been harsh on itself, recognizing the strain upon the law system in a nation that has lost its central ethos and is, therefore, running to formalized systems for redress or protection.

The adversary character of the legal process has also evoked much criticism—a system Roscoe Pound, former dean of the Harvard Law School, described as a "contentious procedure." Critics of this gladiator-lawyer process have cataloged a series of complaints.

The process particularly favors the powerful. If justice is to be a battle, then they win who fight hardest, or, at least, longest. Those with resources, those with access, are best equipped for the ordeal of a lawsuit.

Others have noted with some despair the tactics of the adversary legal process: character assassination, dredging up the worst aspects of the opponent while hiding one's own faults. This sort of thing finally disgusts Ted and Joanna Kramer: "I never thought he'd use that, believe me, Ted," protests Joanna when Ted complains of her lawyer's exaggerated use of an incident. "The lowest, Joanna. The lowest . . ."

Many complain of the rigidity of the system, the tendency of law to become trapped in its own traditions and encumbered with procedures and rules that no longer facilitate justice. Law becomes technique and ritual: a sort of game for the initiated. Still others criticize the system for its focus on blame and fault. Someone wins. Someone loses. The adversary system contributes to procedures and substantive laws that mirror the images of battle and warfare.

Anne Strick, author of *Injustice for All,* points to the frequency of the "terms of weaponry, of injury, of extermination" found in books written by attorneys:

"... to *demolish* the effectiveness of the key witness. . . ."

" ... by *annihilating* the key witness. . . ."

"Cross-examination is the most *potent weapon* known. . . ."

"... it is best to *attack* indirectly. . . ."

Norbert Savay, in his book *The Art of Trial,* is more direct: "A student of the art of advocacy and of the legal contest can profit immensely by a deep and protracted study of war strategy. . . ."

Christians ought to be particularly concerned about a system that rarely focuses on causes. The court seldom looks at why conflict has occurred, how it may be permanently resolved, or how genuine peace may be established. Indeed the system is not just imperfect. At times it is disastrous. It frequently fosters further alienation and diverts the attention of litigants from liberating self-assessment, confession, and forgiveness.

One of the authors of this book recently visited a tobacco auction for the first time, watching with amazement the auctioneer's rapid movement among the piles of tobacco as buyers signaled their bids. On leaving he remarked, "This must be how a layman feels when he goes to court. He senses something important has happened, but he hasn't the vaguest idea what!" It is that sense of being an outsider, a possible victim, that increasingly prevails. It is not "my" justice system. I do not sense "due process." I am not an actor. I only sit. And pay . . . and wait.

Jerold Auerbach capsulized much of this critique of law:

> The bar like the church relies upon mysterious language and procedures to instill reverence and to remove itself from the people. The courtroom is our cathedral, where contemporary passion plays are enacted. . . . As the priest mediated between man and God for the salvation of souls, so the lawyer manipulates a different form of life after death (through trusts and wills). In the twentieth century, as in the fifteenth, form has superseded substance. Now it is justice, the secular equivalent of salvation, which is sold for a fee. Now it is lawyers who corrupt the temple.[1]

If one finds Auerbach a little rough, the words of Judge Learned Hand are not much kinder: "As a litigant, I should dread a lawsuit beyond almost anything else short of sickness and death."

THE LIMITS OF LAW

Former Harvard jurisprudential scholar Lon Fuller once pointed out that human relationships could be viewed on a scale ranging from intimacy to hostility. Fuller then suggested that formal legal process was really designed only to handle the middle range of relationships, and that the legal system is ill equipped and inept at dealing with relationships characterized by high degrees of hostility and/or intimacy.

Fuller's suggestion is striking because we are seeing how often modern courts are immersed precisely in issues that have an emotional content of intimacy and hostility. Consider the explosion of family disputes, domestic law, legal issues with high moral content. It can come as no surprise that statistics in some jurisdictions indicate that less than 20 percent of court-mandated custody solutions are observed by the parents for more than a few years. The court has apparently been unable to deal with the heart of the dispute, and its imposed judicial solution has been unacceptable or unmanageable.

Another interesting factor in Fuller's observation is that the church is quite able to deal with hostility and intimacy. After all, the Gospel is built on basic perceptions about hostility (sin, judgment, alienation) and intimacy (love, grace, reconciliation, forgiveness). The Gospel is aimed at hostile persons, inviting them to experience grace and love. Jesus moves comfortably in environments of hostility and intimacy.

THE LEGITIMACY OF LAW

In spite of the severe criticisms about the ineffectiveness and failures of the present legal system, the courts are still an important and ordained institution in our public life. Law is vital to the structure of our freedoms. Our nation was founded in part to secure a public order built upon law and not upon the whims of autocrats and despots. The administration of a just order through law allows a society to preserve the best of its traditions and values. Law provides a structure of predictability for commercial and oth-

▶25

er relationships, and it protects life and property against mere power. Our legal system is heavily criticized precisely because it is so central to our ordered liberties.

Lawyers often bear the brunt of this criticism, some surely deserved. Even our jokes often have lawyers on the receiving end. This story is typical. Two men were walking through a cemetery when they noticed a gravestone with the inscription: Here lies a Christian and a lawyer. One commented, "Sure must be hard up for land around these parts, burying two men in one grave."

Many lawyers, however, have deep commitments to justice. They encourage the highest ethical standards in their profession and on the part of those they counsel. Not all lawyers can be characterized as "hired guns." Lawyers can and do call on clients, both personal and corporate, to operate not merely on the edges of the law, but within the full moral framework the law was intended to encourage. Chief Justice Warren Burger declared that lawyers "can be healers." Indeed the legal profession offers unique opportunities for resisting the destructive litigation of our day.

While we believe the courts are not the proper place for disputes among believers, they nevertheless provide effective means for assuring civil liberties, calling government and private institutions to accountability, protecting constitutional freedoms and structures, administering the criminal law, and resolving myriad issues that emerge in a complex, pluralistic society. The judicial system and legal profession have many public servants who struggle for justice and care deeply about the failure of the very system they minister in. They need our support.

But we must not expect the legal structures to exhibit the full range of spiritual and human concerns that characterize our particular Christian commitments; the legal structures are, after all, institutions of a secular state. They will omit, for example, the biblical foundation of law in God's righteousness, and its relation to salvation and reconciliation. That does not mean, however, that the state's concern for justice as fairness is wrong. Nor does it mean that Christians should remove themselves from the secular system.

Rather, in our involvement we should remember two things. First, our commitment to God as Creator includes a commitment to seeing his will done in creation—in cultures, communities, neighborhoods, families, and between individuals.

Secondly, our commitment to God as King includes a commitment to the governments he has ordained wherever and whenever we can. We will pray for judges and other persons in authority, will encourage and implement reforms, and will demand like the prophets of old that there be justice for the poor, the widow, and the orphan—those without power, influence, or access.

As we seek peaceful and healing ways of dealing with issues of justice and equity, we contribute to and model a redemptive lifestyle. For we believe that only then can any culture or society, however constituted, long endure.

3 SHOOT-OUT AT OK CORRAL

To dwell above with saints we love,
  That will indeed be glory;
To dwell below with saints we know,
  Well, that's a different story.

This wry piece of folk wisdom reflects a truth that no student of church history or member of a local church body can remain ignorant of for long. The Scriptures in their brilliant realism show us life as it actually was: full of conflict.

Prophets were in conflict with kings. Greek Christians struggled with Hebrew Christians (Acts 6). The New Testament church dealt with serious conflicts at a conference in Jerusalem (Acts 13). Paul challenged Peter over his prejudice in Galatians 2, and Paul and Barnabas disagreed so seriously over John Mark that they separated (Acts 15). Tribes, brothers, cities, religious subdivisions, disciples—all had conflicts.

We are obviously not living in the real world if we think that Christians can avoid conflict. In fact, we will be seriously misguided if we espouse a concept of peace that, by definition, seeks to avoid conflict at all costs. Nowhere in the Bible is it taught that we should avoid all conflict. Nor are models given us of saints who always shunned conflict.

Dr. James Mallory, author of *The Kink and I,* says, "People seem to assume that conflict is inherently bad or that the ideal life would be conflict free. Anybody that is conflict free, I would suspect, is not experiencing growth. . . . The important changes in us take place within the framework of struggle."

While, indeed, some conflict emerges directly from sin, in many cases the real biblical challenge is what we do with our conflicts. The concern of Scripture is not so much that we may have conflict but with the way we respond.

In many cases conflict is healthy and necessary. It may reflect genuine and important differences in values and goals, or differences in means to achieve goals. It may emerge from legitimate concerns for justice toward individuals or groups. In these sorts of cases conflict is simply evidence that we are alive, sensitive, and concerned. To seek to ignore and eliminate such conflict would be to remove a vital opportunity for sharing, interaction, and mutual challenge.

At other times conflict seems more directly related to human sin, or what one author called "unvarnished human cussedness." Paul's list of the works of the flesh in Galatians 5:20 includes not only adultery and idolatry, but "hatred, variance . . . wrath, strife, . . . envyings." These are contrary to the life in the Spirit, which rejects "provoking one another." Even when willful sin is not the direct cause of the conflict, the controversy draws out our competitiveness, ego insecurities, and sensitivities.

The tragedy is that many disagreements that begin with legitimate differences, or simply out of misunderstandings, quickly degenerate into massive conflicts, which escalate to include personal attacks, attempts to gain alliances and allies, and a collection of hurts. Before long the real issue, which began the process, is lost.

Ron Kraybill in *Repairing the Breach* has an instructive list of eight ways to turn a simple disagreement into a feud, a model of how not to respond to conflict:

1. Be sure to develop and maintain a healthy fear of conflict, letting your own feelings build up so you are in an explosive frame of mind.
2. If you must state your concerns, be as vague and general as possible. Then the other person cannot do anything practical to change the situation.
3. Assume you know all the facts and you are totally right. The use of a clinching Bible verse is helpful. Speak prophetically for truth and justice; do most of the talking.
4. With a touch of defiance, announce your willingness to talk with anyone who wishes to discuss the problem with you. But do not take steps to initiate such conversation.
5. Latch tenaciously onto whatever evidence you can find that shows the other person is merely jealous of you.
6. Judge the motivation of the other party on any previous experience that showed failure or unkindness. Keep track of any angry words.
7. If the discussion should, alas, become serious, view the issue as a win/lose struggle. Avoid possible solutions and go for total victory and unconditional surrender. Don't get too many options on the table.
8. Pass the buck! If you are about to get

cornered into a solution, indicate you are
without power to settle: you need your
partner, spouse, bank, whatever.

Pastoral counselor David Augsburger describes a process that is diametrically op-
posed to such game playing in *Caring
Enough to Confront.* He proposes a posture
that takes the conflict and the person seriously and values the issues and the relationship enough to be direct, honest, and caring.
This approach refuses to seek domination
through control and power, refuses to settle
into a long cold war, and refuses to withdraw into isolation. It chooses instead to
risk.

After all, conflict can offer some unique
opportunities for God's Word to become
more alive and for us to grow in the Spirit.
Conflict may clarify important issues so that
we can all become more faithful and learn
through the body of Christ. Conflict, rightly
processed, may move superficial relationships into deep friendships. A genuine unity
can actually emerge from conflict because
we have encountered each other seriously
and not just passively and superficially,
which is so often the case in what is touted
as "fellowship."

Conflict is likewise a tremendous opportunity to practice the presence of Christ: to
learn patience (Rom. 5:3, James 1:3), gentleness, meekness, and humility (2 Cor. 12:7-
10), honesty, forthrightness, and truth-
speaking with love.

Believers ministering in legal peacemaking
assume we are not afraid of conflict. We do
not deny it, hide it, camouflage it. Rather we
acknowledge and deal with conflict openly,
hopefully, and directly.

Till now, Christians have had only two
choices when serious legal conflict emerged.

One was to simply swallow hard and "forget it," which is easier said than done! You might spiritualize this choice by saying that this was forgiveness, but it was often simply a lack of will to pursue the matter further. The anger and sense of being cheated were still there. Unresolved feelings smouldered and affected attitudes, spiritual vitality, and often health.

The other alternative was to hire an attorney and "go after them." The stated purpose was to obtain justice, but often the underlying motivation was a desire for revenge. Someone ought to pay. So emotional energy and not a little money went to support this modern version of the shoot-out at OK Corral. As in the Old West, the opponents would gather in the center of the city, each side well armed, and fire away while the townsfolk watched. The old system was called "frontier justice"; the new system is called "litigation." The process and victims are about the same, except that today the bullets are more expensive.

Churches usually select the first option and run from conflict. They seek, sometimes at all costs, to avoid conflicts. They don't want to own them at all. They wish they'd go away. They have enough troubles of their own without becoming involved in other people's. How long has it been since you've seen a church court in action, or had the Board of Elders or the deacons act as mediators or arbitrators to resolve a commercial dispute in the community?

A representative study in one medium-size metropolitan area revealed that churches rarely acted either alone or in concert with other churches to reconcile legal conflict. In fact, pastors were generally unaware of lawsuits their members were involved in, and no disciplinary procedures or even counseling mechanisms existed to resolve legal disputes between believers. In that community alone it was estimated that 8,000 cases each year involved persons on both sides who called themselves Christians—with legal fees reaching perhaps $12 million.

In the few instances where churches had tried to act as mediators, they had been unable to work through the conflict. Instead they tried to settle the matter quickly with a "prayer and a compromise"—hardly the reconciliation the Scripture invites.

The church's abdication of responsibility is particularly tragic because it is, as we have noted, uniquely gifted as a healer and peacemaker. Consider also the powerful biblical commitment to justice as the work of God's righteousness.

The church has been commissioned to take a peacemaking role in the lives of believers. Though the Scriptures have been clear about this, the church has largely ignored that responsibility. Now, we are again being called to faithfulness.

PART 2 **THE CHALLENGE OF RECONCILIATION**

4 TELL IT TO THE CHURCH

Now that we have glimpsed the legal dilemma that exists within our society, let us propose an alternative to the court system: a biblical ministry of conflict resolution and reconciliation. Here the Scriptures are especially powerful. As usual they give us more than just great foundational truths for living; they reach down into our lives and provide specific direction, a "light to our paths." Matthew 18:15-17 suggests that even in our conflicts we should implement our fellowship and maintain the witness and unity of the church:

Moreover, if thy brother shall trespass against thee, go and tell him his fault between thee and him alone: if he shall hear thee, thou has gained thy brother.

But if he will not hear thee, then take with thee one or two more, that in the mouth of two or three witnesses every word may be established.

And if he shall neglect to hear them, tell it unto the church: but if he neglect to hear the church, let him be unto thee as an heathen man and a publican.

In this passage our Lord suggests a three-step process for dealing with situations where one believes another has "trespassed" against him:

1. Go to your brother in private.
2. Take one or two others along with you.
3. Tell it unto the church.

We are primarily concerned with the second and third steps, but the first step is equally critical to the healing process.

GO TO YOUR BROTHER

If you believe you have been wronged by your brother, go to him in private with your claim. It is the same counsel contained in the biblical admonition "agree with thine adversary quickly, while thou art with him in the way" or the counsel of Paul in Ephesians 4, "Let not the sun go down upon your wrath" (v. 26).

How often do you hear a Christian complain about an alleged wrong instigated by another? When asked if they have talked to the other party, they admit they have not. Before the Christian Conciliation Service (CCS) intercedes in a dispute, the complaining party must have sought to fulfill this first step.

Note that it is the party who presumes himself innocent who is challenged to take the initiative to resolve the issue. It may be that the genuinely innocent party is better positioned to move toward the guilty party. It certainly models precisely what Christ has done for us. The guilty party is similarly charged with taking the initiative in Matthew 5:

But I say unto you, That whosoever is angry with his brother without a cause shall be in danger of the judgment: and whosoever shall say to his brother, Raca, shall be in danger of the council: but whosoever shall say, Thou fool, shall be in danger of hell fire.

Therefore if thou bring thy gift to the altar, and there rememberest that thy brother hath ought against thee;

Leave there thy gift before the altar, and go thy way; first be reconciled to thy brother, and then come and offer thy gift (vv. 22-24).

In a recent case called to the attention of the Christian Conciliation Service, a creditor called to complain that a Christian organization had failed to pay an account considerably past due and had failed to answer mail or return phone calls. When we contacted the Christian group, the leader refused to call the creditor to discuss the situation, alleging that they were innocent and were not going to "waste a dime" to talk to the business. They presumed their innocence precluded any responsibility on their part. The Scripture we have quoted from Matthew 18 suggests the contrary.

A distraught woman was sued for a considerable sum of money owed on a note she and another party (who was unavailable and not party to the suit) had signed. The woman was losing sleep and felt helpless because she was without immediate funds to repay the loan. But she had not spoken to the businessman who had brought the suit against her six months earlier. Taking the mediator's advice, she went to see the other party. She shared with him her anxiety, fear, and inability to repay. In an hour or so the issue was resolved.

All too often this first step of going to the other party in private is omitted. One may complain to others, but rarely go directly to the other and express the complaint or concern. John Alexander in his book, *Practical Criticism: Giving It and Taking It* affirms the need for this private encounter, which is direct, specific, and truthful.

It is not insignificant that the Scriptures suggest that this first step should be in private. Before others are brought into the conflict, before witnesses or the church are included, the parties should seek a reconciliation on a personal and private basis. In such initial meetings, friends or advisors may, in fact, impede reconciliation. Others who wish to rush in quickly might note the counsel of Proverbs 26:17: "He who meddles in a quarrel not his own is like one who takes a passing dog by the ears" (RSV).

TAKE ALONG WITNESSES

If the private meeting is unsuccessful, Jesus indicates the aggrieved party should take one or two others as witnesses and visit the other party again. One aspect of this step may be to provide witnesses to the alleged wrong and the unwillingness of the other party to face the wrong. Another aspect, however, seems to be the encouragement from friends and colleagues of the disputing parties. One commentator has even suggested that the friends should be those of the other party and not of oneself. In any event the intent is clearly to seek to utilize other members of the family of Christ to encourage, and, if necessary, call one or both of the parties to account. Perhaps the one or two witnesses are like mediators and conciliators.

TELL IT TO THE CHURCH

This step is the significant suggestion of this text; it insists that the church is to be the judge and the forum for resolving disputes between members of the believing community.

Persons may think that their legal disputes are personal, unrelated to spiritual affairs or, at least, irrelevant to the body of believers. After all, what do church people know about child custody, medical malpractice, mechanic's liens, and insurance claims? Yet the Word declares this is not so. These disputes belong to the community of God's people. In 1 Corinthians 6:1-5 Paul criticizes the believers of Corinth for using the secular courts to resolve disputes between members of the Christian community:

Dare any of you, having a matter against another, go to law before the unjust, and not before the saints? Do ye not know that the saints shall judge the world? And if the world shall be judged by you, are ye unworthy to judge the smallest matters? . . . If then ye have judgments of things pertaining to this life, set them to judge who are least esteemed in the church. I speak to your shame. Is it so, that there is not a wise man among you? . . .

Paul is not talking about theological disputes. These are not disputes about church affairs, but disputes that we would characterize today as commercial claims, tort claims—perhaps landlord-tenant claims and neighborhood issues. The church has jurisdiction not simply over religious litigation, but over all disputes between believers.

Why should the church at Corinth get involved in resolving commercial disputes between believers? Because she is gifted as a judge, Paul says. She will ultimately judge the angels. She has in her body the gifts of wisdom and discernment necessary for just and righteous judgment. Paul also insists that to go to the secular court brings shame on the body. It destroys the witness of fellowship and unity. It pits members against each other in the public forum.

In fact, it is so disgraceful that it would be better to be defrauded than to go to the courts. Defrauded! That is powerful language. It assumes that one may have been ripped off, cheated, abused. No light matter this. Yet it would be better to suffer wrong and loss than destroy the role and witness of the church, Paul says.

This teaching of Paul in 1 Corinthians 6 and that of our Lord in Matthew 18 combine to create a powerful demand on both the church and believers. The church should be prepared to be an instrument of healing and reconciliation. It should use its offices to encourage—even perhaps to insist—that its members utilize the gifts of the body in resolving disputes.

Yet, this has not been done. Churches have been largely unprepared, even, perhaps, unwilling to act. Certainly they are unwilling to exercise their spiritual authority to call persons to faithfulness in this area.

Besides the church's hesitancy to enter conflict, some practical considerations have kept the church away from legal disputes. One major problem is that most disputes between church members do not involve members from the same church. This is especially so in the area of commercial and tort claims. Who is to judge a dispute between members of First Baptist and First Methodist? How are the parties to know if the other is a believer? It has depressed us to note how commonly one party who may be willing to follow the principles of Matthew 18 just assumes that the other party is not Christian and would be totally unwilling to submit the dispute to a panel of believers.

In the first century, the believing community in a city was all part of one worshiping, sharing family. They knew each other and had some sense of accountability to the same pastoral and spiritual leadership. Today the believing community is not only in different buildings, but often does not share many experiences of prayer and spiritual growth.

But an exploration of the Corinthian passage reveals that it does not suggest that the whole church hear the dispute. Nor does the Matthean text require a congregational meeting to air the dispute. The Corinthian passage seems to suggest that the body appoint some individuals who are gifted and called to peacemaking as reconcilers and mediators. The church in Matthew 18 and the saints in 1 Corinthians 6 should not be seen exclusively in terms of the local congregation, but in terms of the whole body. That is critical if the church is to have an effective ministry today. It must include not only local church structures and systems, but other entities that allow the larger body of Christ to deal with disputes involving persons who are members of different fellowships.

A further conclusion from these texts is that the resolution of disputes ought to include far more than lawyers or others acquainted with law. Since it is a ministry of the whole church, it will include not only the powerful but the "least" as Paul suggests: all classes, professions, and perspectives. Reconciling is a universal call. The Scriptures have given all of us the task of being "agents of reconciliation."

THE CHURCH'S AUTHORITY IN SETTLING DISPUTES

What is especially striking in the context of the verses in Matthew are the passages that immediately follow the invitation to "tell it to the church."

Note the promise of Matthew 18:18: "Whatsoever ye shall bind on earth shall be bound in heaven: and whatsoever ye shall

loose on earth shall be loosed in heaven."
Read this verse in the context of the gathered community seeking to render a decision
in a dispute between believers. Or in light of
a child-custody battle, a contract dispute, or
a personal-injury claim.

What authority! Imagine the power Jesus
gives to the church to act with finality in
judging between believers. It is unappealable—even to heaven itself. Jesus indicates
that heaven will stand by and affirm the decisions the church makes when, in faithfulness, it resolves disputes. This also means
that the believer who might be tempted to
complain about the decision or feel it was
not just is without recourse.

Is the church then infallible when it decides cases? Not at all. The decision may not
perfectly reflect justice, but it is still final. It
is the best the church could do, and the
Lord wants his people to accept that and
move on. Reconciliation is more fundamental
than being "right"!

In a highly charged custody dispute resolved by the CCS, a natural mother contested with the adoptive parents over custody
rights to a child. Such disputes are tradition-
ally bitter struggles. What issue could be
more tense, more emotional? Sam Ericsson,
the member of CCS who handled the dispute, recalls the case:

Prior to delivery, Julie (the names we will
use are fictitious) was under the impression
that she had up to a year to decide whether
to finalize the adoption. She did not know
that the law in her state limited the decision
time to six months after placement of the
child.

The adopting couple (let's call them the
Olsons) picked up little Jeremy from the hospital a few days after birth. Julie never saw

her baby. Seven months later, the state social worker asked Julie to sign the final adoption papers. Julie indicated that after much prayer, she had decided to keep her baby. She felt that this clearly was God's will for her and the child.

After the social worker advised the Olsons of the decision, they met with Julie, but were unsuccessful in their efforts to persuade her to change her mind.

The Olsons went to see an attorney who recommended court proceedings, noting that Julie had acted too late to revoke her placement. In view of their belief that God had truly placed Jeremy in their home, the Olsons instructed their lawyer to proceed with court action against Julie.

Julie's pastor asked me to refer her to a lawyer, which I did.

I later called the attorneys, both of whom were Christians, and discussed with them the option of submitting the matter to the church.

Neither Julie's nor the Olsons' attorneys had ever been involved in this type of proceeding, but both of them felt it was worth considering. Admittedly, we were all somewhat nervous about submitting such a weighty matter to a relatively new procedure. However, we were convinced that even though following the principles set forth in God's Word might involve risks, God always honors such efforts.

Julie and the Olsons agreed to proceed and to be morally bound by the unanimous decision of a panel of three Christian attorneys who would be asked to make the decision. All of the attorneys were above reproach and met the qualifications of 1 Timothy 3 and Titus 1. They also were highly respected as lawyers.

Shortly before the hearing, Mr. Olson, a

competent Bible student, submitted a lengthy study of his understanding of the scriptural teaching on children, parenting, and adoption.

He asked that this material be submitted to the panel for their consideration. The paper left little doubt as to the "right" result.

Clearly, the panel should be advised of the biblical teaching on relevant subjects, but I felt that for either party to do the biblical research would most likely place the Olsons at a significant advantage over Julie who had less training and competence in Scripture. We therefore asked a well-respected seminary professor to provide the relevant scriptural input and to serve as an "expert" witness if necessary. Each side was free to comment on the professor's paper and reply to each other's comments.

The night before the hearing, I was both excited and nervous. Everything had gone extremely well thus far. To a great extent, the parties and the attorneys had entrusted most of the "orchestrating" to me. For example, the parties had never met the three lawyers on the panel. They had simply taken my word that these men were wise, impartial, and above reproach. Thus, they agreed to be bound by a decision concerning their future relationship with their child based primarily on my assurances that the panel was indeed competent and Spirit-led.

Now we were ready for the hearing.

In order to place the somewhat informal proceedings in proper biblical context and reduce the more common "adversary" tone of legal proceedings, I opened with the following remarks:

"As Christians, our perspective on life is different than that of the non-Christian. Simply stated, we believe that Scripture speaks with authority in all areas of faith and practice. The fact that an issue is difficult and even painful to resolve does not change our belief in the supremacy of Scripture. Therefore, before we proceed with hearing one another, we need to ask ourselves three questions: Why are we here? How should these proceedings be conducted? and What must be the dominant quality displayed in these proceedings?" Each question was answered by reading pertinent Scripture: 1 Corinthians 6:1-11, Philippians 2:1-8, and 1 Corinthians 13.

"In summary, therefore, why are we here today? Because God's Word says this is the procedure to follow. Second, how should these proceedings be conducted? As if Christ himself was presiding here today. And third, what should be the dominant quality throughout these proceedings? As Christ said, By this all men will know that you are my disciples, if you have love for one another."

After prayer, Julie and the Olsons and their counsel shared the facts (legal and biblical principles) and other points that they wished to present. It was a unique experience for all of us as we saw the hearing unfold and the Lord's leading. Absent was the self-serving, often hostile and bitter, arguing and accusations. Instead, everyone strove to put the other's interests above his or her own. We all wanted God's will for this child.

In fact, often during the two-hour hearing, each side voluntarily pointed out the strengths it felt the other party had. Even their lawyers presented points supportive not only of their own clients but of the other side.

The destiny of Jeremy was at issue. Yet, at the end of the proceeding, the mothers embraced—both feeling that the hearing had been conducted in a way honoring to

God. Indeed, true reconciliation had taken place. Incidentally, both parties felt that the other side had won.

About three weeks after the hearing, the panel gave its decision. In their opinion both parties would make a fine home for a child. As to this child, however, the panel unanimously held that the Olsons should keep Jeremy.[1]

The "loser," in this case the natural mother, did not necessarily agree with the decision. In fact she still felt she should have been awarded custody. But she knew the arbitrators had made the best decision they knew how. She had been heard by loving and sensitive fellow believers. The church had been faithful to the biblical mandate, had spoken, and therefore, that was the end of it. She accepted the decision as final—and even gave a gift to the conciliation ministry.

The principle of our Lord's endorsement of the decisions of the church is reinforced in Matthew 18:19: "If two of you shall agree on earth as touching any thing that they shall ask, it shall be done for them of my Father which is in heaven."

Verse 20 is equally powerful. It declares, "Where two or three are gathered together in my name, there am I in the midst of them." How often that verse has been quoted to guarantee divine presence at small group Bible studies and prayer meetings. Christ is indeed present in such gatherings. But the text actually suggests a very specific context for his presence: when the church seeks to be a judge and reconciler. Christ's wisdom, his love, his authority, his power are available. No wonder there is no appeal to heaven—for heaven itself is there.

The powerful calling of the church to this ministry suggests that the church has failed when it refuses to teach and discipline its members to be reconcilers. It is incumbent on the church to instruct its leadership to discipline those who refuse to obey the mandates of Scripture: expulsion from leadership, censure, rebuke, and expulsion from the church.

MEDIATION AND ARBITRATION AS A BIBLICAL PROCESS

Mediation and arbitration are systems by which parties agree to submit the issues between them to one or more persons to assist in resolving the dispute. The power and role of the mediators or arbitrators derive from the agreement of the parties to submit the dispute to them. Mediation and arbitration agreements typically spell out the authority of the conciliator.

The function of the mediator is to assist the parties to come to an agreement by listening carefully, encouraging the full exploration of the issues, effective and honest communication, and perhaps suggesting areas of potential compromise or resolution. The mediator has no power to decide, but can help the parties come to a decision themselves.

The arbitrator, however, is empowered by the parties to render a decision. This decision may, by prior agreement of the parties, be only advisory, with the parties free to accept or reject it. Or the parties may agree in advance that the decision will be binding. In such an event the decision of the arbitrator is usually final and enforceable in a secular court.

When one reviews the role of the church suggested in Matthew 18 and 1 Corinthians 6, it seems evident that roles of mediation and arbitration are contemplated. The church is clearly to function as a mediator. In fact the word *mediator* is used to describe the work of Christ in bridging the gap between God and man. Christ is the one mediator (Hebrews 9:15), and we are to follow his example.

But it is clear that the believing community has a greater role than merely acting as a sort of middleman to encourage solutions. Both Matthew 18 and 1 Corinthians 6 contemplate the authority of the church to render judgments on the matters at dispute. Paul speaks of the capacity of even the least to make just judgments, and Matthew 18 promises that the authority of heaven stands behind the decisions. The church functions, therefore, as an arbitrator, whose decisions are spiritually binding on the disputing believers.

Some secular dispute resolution programs involve a conciliation approach, which is a mixture of mediation and arbitration, usually referred to by the abbreviation "med/arb." In this structure, the conciliator begins with an effort to assist the parties in arriving at their own resolution. However, if the parties seem unable to come to a settlement between themselves, then the conciliator is empowered to render a decision. Such a model seems to reflect the process of Matthew 18 where others assist in a resolution. Failing that, the church has the responsibility to decide the issue.

Though the models of mediation and arbitration are expressive of the biblical role, the secular equivalents are not totally transferable. There are, in fact, significant differences between the secular processes and the role of the church, as we shall note in the following sections.

5

THE ALBUQUERQUE PROJECT: A PERSONAL TESTIMONY

"God wants to heal you, Laury." The words seemed strange in the clinical, detached world of the psychiatric ward of St. Patrick's Hospital in Missoula, Montana. Although I am now national coordinator of the Christian Conciliation Service and executive director of the CCS of New Mexico, on August 19, 1976, I had been admitted to this hospital because of my addiction to drugs and alcohol.

Shortly before my commitment, I had started reading my Bible again and seeking God. But the first doctor I talked to in the hospital had assured me that he, too, had gone through this "religious phase."

"It's a dead-end street, you know," he'd said. "You can't lean on crutches like religion. They'll just compound your problems."

But Penny, committed by her husband as a "religious fanatic," a young woman who seemed to be the sanest person there, had listened to me with real understanding.

"God wants to heal you, Laury, but you need Christ in your life," she challenged. "I'll be praying for you."

As I watched her take communion in the hospital the next day, it seemed that Christ was speaking to my heart: "This is my body, given for you. . . . This is my blood, shed for you."

But I was not ready for that step yet. My downward spiral continued, and by October of 1976 I ended up as a patient at Massachusetts General Hospital. I had worked as legal counsel in the Massachusetts Department of Mental Health when I was a graduate student at Harvard seven years before. Now, ironically, I was a patient. My wife had left me and was seeking divorce; my career as a successful trial lawyer seemed shattered. I had brought sorrow to those who loved me, embarrassment to myself, and worse, I was a prisoner of drugs and alcohol.

No one, least of all myself, would have imagined that a young man who had been raised in a good Christian home would find himself caught in such a whirlpool of self-destruction at the age of thirty-three. Certainly my success had at one time seemed secure. I had graduated first in my class from law school, and, after my graduate study at Harvard, had established a law practice in my native Montana, representing claimants in personal injury and malpractice cases. I had become a member of the board of governors of the Montana Trial Lawyers Association, taught courses in law at the University of Montana, and was offered a prestigious position at an eastern law school. I had carried my 6'5" frame proudly throughout the "Land of the Big Sky."

In a few short years of practice I had achieved the goals that were important to me: a good wife and two children, a huge mansion on a hill, plenty of money, a good job, professional recognition, and prestige.

However, as I look back, the words that Jesus spoke to the lawyers of his day were applicable to me: "How terrible for you, teachers of the Law. . . . You hypocrites! You are like whitewashed tombs, which look fine on the outside but are full of bones and decaying corpses on the inside. In the same way, on the outside you appear good to everybody, but inside you are full of hypocrisy and sins" (Matt. 23:27, TEV).

I fit that pattern. Inside, my life was characterized by rebelliousness, confused priorities, and spiritual emptiness. Slowly I began to realize how helpless I was in dealing with people's problems. They came to me saying they wanted justice, but I sensed bitterness and a spirit of revenge. They came with a profound sense of loss, in the midst of a crisis. Some had lost jobs and money, others health, but I had little to offer. In fact, I suggested more conflict, more bitterness. I encouraged them to think of "getting even." But I put it in terms of serving justice and not letting the other party "get away with it."

I also encouraged a fighting spirit and sought for compensable injuries, focusing on my clients' rights, often at the expense of very important relationships that were fractured during the course of the legal conflict. I grew increasingly aware that I was not touching the real cause of conflict, for underneath the lawsuits and the petitions for justice were spirits of anger, resentment, unforgiveness—and behind these were problems of pride and unbelief.

The more I sensed these problems the less satisfying my own life became. I found that I couldn't even follow what good advice I gave to others. I was powerless and gradu-

ally hopeless. I began to search for meaning
in the occult, and then in the diversions of
life: planes, motorcycles, all-terrain vehicles.
I sought adventure, traveling in Mexico and
South America. I began to represent exciting
and powerful interests and groups: people
involved in media and crime. But these "exciting people" only brought more suffering.
Before long I found myself addicted to drugs
and alcohol.

After six years of legal practice, my marriage was in serious trouble. In desperation,
my wife told me one day, "You know, Laury,
you're becoming just like the people you
represent—angry, isolated, trying to com-
pensate for your loneliness and emptiness
with money and material things."

She was right. When you consistently represent a certain kind of client—when you
practice speaking for them, thinking for
them, defending them—you become like
them.

My life had rapidly deteriorated until I
was committed to the mental hospital in
Montana where friends hoped the counseling and psychiatric skills could restore me to
health. But neither there nor in Massachusetts did I find the relief I needed.

Shortly after being released, uncured, from
Massachusetts General Hospital, God finally
broke into my life. As so often happens, the
Scriptures only reveal their special power
when they touch a life that desperation and
loss has finally opened.

In November of 1976 I moved to St. Pe-
tersburg, Florida, where the Lord began to
speak to me about the need for repentance,
confession, and forgiveness. The psychia-
trists had told me that I had a serious problem with the guilt I felt, which had to be put
behind me. One day, alone in my apartment
reading the Bible, I confessed my sins to the

Lord, and I experienced forgiveness—a release from this overbearing guilt—although I still struggled with my need for drugs and liquor.

Before Christmas that year, I moved to the Mexican desert just south of the Texas border to be alone and think. However, my mind was often confused by drugs, and I was still bothered by my past excursions into the occult. That disturbed period ended suddenly on February 14, 1977, with an automobile accident, which brought me so close to death that a local Catholic priest said the last rites over me.

The Mexican authorities called my father in Montana who arrived the next day and effected my transfer from the hospital in Piedras Negras to San Antonio, Texas, where I learned I was bleeding to death from massive internal hemorrhaging.

Yet I was so depressed and my thinking was so distorted by the morphine and cocaine with which I was being sedated that I refused the surgery necessary to save my life. I even threatened the doctors with malpractice suits if they proceeded. Only outside intervention saved the life that I was beyond caring for. Some months before, I had given my father power of attorney to handle my affairs, and he used it to authorize the necessary medical care.

Shortly after I was released from my two-month hospital stay, the Lord showed me that I needed to do more than accept the forgiveness that Jesus provided through his death on the cross. I needed to give Jesus what I had given my father, a power of attorney in my life.

I dimly remember my father weeping in the hospital room as I rebuffed the doctors, and I also remember realizing how much this man must love me. Now it seemed that

Jesus was saying, "Laury, I'm sitting by the side of your life as your father sat by your bedside. I want to help you, but I can't until you put me first in your life; I need complete power of attorney."

And when I did that, the Lord healed me spiritually, mentally, and physically. I was delivered from the serious addictions that had held me prisoner.

That summer Dorothy, a friend who was trained as an Episcopal priest and counselor, mediated between my wife and me. I came to know firsthand the power that a third person can bring into a seemingly irreconcilable conflict. The power of Jesus Christ healed the brokenness and conflict within my own family, and my wife and I were reunited. But I did not know what I would do professionally when I joined her in Albuquerque, New Mexico, where she was living. All I knew was that the healing and reconciliation I had experienced were desperately needed in the legal world—and elsewhere. Businesses needed them. Injured people, hurt people, angry people needed them.

I joined a small group of attorneys who began to meet for breakfast and pray for the Lord's strength and direction to follow the ministry of reconciliation suggested in Matthew 18 and 1 Corinthians 6. John Robb, Jr., a senior partner in the Rodey law firm, was particularly instrumental in encouraging and inspiring me to initiate a conciliation program.

We had noted the significant level of legal conflicts in Albuquerque—a city of approximately four hundred thousand. In 1978, there had been about sixteen thousand lawsuits in the county. By 1980, when the program of Christian conciliation was formally begun, the number of suits had increased to over thirty thousand. Statistically, nearly one in every three adult citizens was involved in a lawsuit each year. Yet 60 percent of the people in the county were members of churches and would call themselves "Christians."

Although many ministries were barely making it for lack of funds, Christians were spending $20 million in legal fees each year in our small county. It seemed clear that these lawsuits represented not only disobedience on the part of the individuals involved, but also on the part of the church as a whole.

We began to talk to pastors in our community and discovered that very few had any experience in resolving church members' legal disputes. In fact, pastors rarely knew when members of their own congregation were involved in lawsuits with other believers—except in domestic cases.

During May of 1980 we conducted a citywide conference at the University of New Mexico Law School. About three hundred people attended to hear recognized leaders in biblical conflict resolution, the chief justice of the New Mexico Supreme Court, the executive director of the New Mexico Inter-Church Agency, the president of the state bar association, and leadership of the Christian Legal Society speak of ways the church could minister to persons in legal conflict.

Shortly after the conference we invited pastors, Christian lawyers, businessmen, counselors, and other leaders in Christian ministry to meet with us and explore ways to implement the challenge of Scripture. A board was created to form a local chapter of the developing Christian Conciliation Service. It consisted of lawyers, businessmen, professional counselors, and people from a variety of other professions and vocations.

The group represented considerable denominational, economic, and racial diversity—all committed to the lordship of Jesus Christ and the authority of Scripture, which we knew could speak to the legal conflicts in our community.

As our group grew, the board began to call the church to faithfulness and set up rules and structures for providing services of mediation and arbitration. A training program was established to equip people to minister in both the CCS and their local churches.

By the summer of 1981 there were over seventy lawyers, seventy pastors, and one hundred laypeople prepared to serve without fee as peacemakers in disputes between Christians, handling over sixty cases a month. Typically, cases were assigned to a team of three mediators, often consisting of a pastor or elder, a lawyer, and a third person with skills related to the area of the dispute (for example, an architect, a contractor, banker, etc.).

Frankly, we were not sure the program would work when we began. We were not motivated by optimism—or even faith in our program. Rather we saw our actions as simple obedience to God; we were driven by a knowledge of what the Lord had done in our own lives, that was coupled with a perception of the destructiveness of the present adversarial legal system.

We have not only seen the resolution of what some might call "small disputes," but major cases including oil lease issues; claims involving large real estate, building, and insurance companies; interstate disputes; criminal cases; domestic disputes over divorce settlements; and custody claims—in some cases involving many millions of dollars. Often we were able to intervene before cases had even been filed. But of more consequence, we have seen relationships healed and people restored to health and joy.

In one case, two Christians involved in a joint sales venture came into bitter conflict over their business. They accused each other of theft of business property, writing bad checks, slander, criminal conspiracy, and a variety of other charges. Both were in counseling, one with a Christian counselor and the other with a Jewish psychiatrist; but the counselors could not deal with the legal issues involved and, indeed, feared that physical violence or litigation would soon follow.

The CCS set up a meeting at a neutral church. Beginning with prayer, the conciliators invited the "God of Abraham, Isaac, and Jacob" to be present, and then encouraged the parties to share what Christ meant in their lives, rather than immediately proceeding to the issues of the dispute.

Within one hour a process of reconciliation began that allowed the parties to completely resolve the financial aspects of their dispute. Confession and forgiveness were followed by the drafting of covenants for the parties' mutual ministry and fellowship.

The Jewish psychiatrist, who had accompanied his client to prevent possible violence, could not believe his eyes, and the mediators themselves were stunned by the speed and completeness of the reconciliation—a process they had, after introductory statements, sat back and watched. The healing power of Christ had moved in the disputants' spirits and lives.

So deep is the need for this sort of ministry in our national life that now over thirty cities are exploring the creation of local programs related to the Christian Conciliation Service. Similar programs already exist in Seattle, Washington, D.C., and Los Angeles. Pastors are eager to see their congregations implement these principles, seminaries are open to teaching in this area, and Christian lawyers are excited about this new dimension to their practice.

We receive many requests to present the details of our program, but one recent invitation was a reminder to me personally of the power of prayer and the faithfulness of our God.

A call came to my home, inviting me to speak to a group of Christian businessmen in a nearby city; they wanted some more information about our program. A week later the representative of the Full Gospel Businessmen's group in that city called to confirm the appointment to speak. Almost as an afterthought, he mentioned that his wife knew me, that in fact she had been praying for me for a long time—ever since she had met me one day in a hospital in Montana.

PART 3 THE DIMENSIONS OF PEACEMAKING

6 SPIRITUAL RESTORATION

Christians can wholeheartedly endorse all efforts to promote peace and justice, regardless of their source or form. But Christian involvement in these efforts should be more than just a Christian attempt to boost secular programs. Christians bring a unique perspective and power to resolving disputes.

A woman recently came to the CCS for mediation in a dispute with a business partner. She had been cheated out of $50,000 by being excluded from sharing in some partnership assets, and she was seeking restitution.

As she discussed the matter with the CCS counselors, she became impressed with the possibility of forgiveness. Forgive the loss of $50,000? Fraud? Theft? Yes, she decided this was possible. So she went with the mediators to her former partner and his wife, people who had avoided her—and she them—for over two years. She told them she knew what they had done, but that she was forgiving them in Jesus. Her former partner broke down in tears, confessed his sin, and asked for her forgiveness. Acknowledging that the assets had been squandered, he declared his intent to return all that he had taken as he was able.

Forgiveness had broken through the alienation and bitterness; it had broken through guilt and sin. Christian mediation and arbitration are not merely Christian involvement in secular programs. They are ministries built around a Christian world view, motivated by a commitment to follow the Lord's example. As such they bring into play some of the great and resounding themes of the Christian life.

RECONCILIATION

Christians who seek to implement Matthew 18 and 1 Corinthians 6 have an enormous task, a goal worthy of the church's ministry. Instead of merely resolving the dispute, their goal is to reconcile the disputing parties.

Consider the biblical principle of reconciliation between God and man. God's purpose was not simply to "settle" the dispute, but to actually create a new and powerful bond.

But of course reconciliation is not only the work of the Son. It is also the work of the believer. Paul declares in 2 Corinthians 5:18, "All this is from God, who through Christ reconciled us to himself and gave us the ministry of reconciliation" (RSV).

The New Testament teaches that Christ not only restored the relationship between God and man, but broke down the walls of hostility and alienation, which are built into our societies like a maze.

In the early church the struggle of reconciliation was acted out primarily in the context of the Jew and gentile who were culturally, religiously, and geographically hostile. Yet Paul can declare in Ephesians 2:11 that though gentiles were indeed aliens, strangers from the covenants, nevertheless "now in Christ Jesus ye who sometimes were far off are made nigh by the blood of Christ. For he is our peace, who hath made both one, and hath broken down the middle wall of partition between us."

Reconciliation reverberates through the New Testament with a threefold theme: a reconciliation that is the work of God to bring man to himself, a reconciliation between man and man, and a ministry of reconciliation, which is given to the church.

Nowhere is this theme more evident than in Jesus' story of a worshiper who brings a lamb to the outer court of the temple to wait for the priest to receive and sacrifice it. Only the most pressing matter could possibly interrupt this solemn act of confession. Yet the worshiper suddenly remembers an unreconciled brother who holds something against him. He leaves his gift and runs quickly to be reconciled, then returns full of peace and joy to offer his sacrifice.

No doctrine ought to be more proclaimed and practiced in our day than reconciliation. We are in an age of individualism, alienation, meaninglessness, and cosmic isolation. We need desperately to hear of a reconciliation that can place man in harmony with the Lord of the universe and give meaning to the chaos and confusion that surround us—the loneliness of sheer technology, existentialism, and materialism. We are also in an age of radical alienation between man and man. This is no mere theology. We can name the signs of the alienation about us: Cambodia, Ireland, Afghanistan, Poland, South Africa. We could also easily name the families and friends whose lives have been touched with the hurt and pain of broken relationships and shattered families. The fact that God can give people a unity and oneness is a liberating truth—one the world strains to hear.

Legal peacemaking ministries by the

church exist not merely to get an "answer" to a legal question (such as who owes whom $500 and when shall they pay it), but to work toward rebuilding relationships so there may be not only justice, but full biblical peace *(shalom)*. The full reconciliation of aliens, enemies, and strangers ends with celebration—of God and each other.

Quick fixes, easy compromises, and "oh, forget its" will not do. There will be real work and real struggle. But in cases where reconciliation occurs, the final relationship will result in a more fundamental spiritual unity than before the break. Now there is more openness, more understanding, and a greater commitment to communication. Business partners who are in a bitter struggle over the remaining assets of a collapsed venture are to emerge as closer spiritual brothers than they were at the height of their success.

In many ministries of reconciliation little more may be done than to sow seeds of peace, which others will have to water and still others harvest. But at least we shall invite the parties to real restoration—to the party God gives for those who are reconciled. And we shall be sure we have not participated in a process that drives people further apart.

FOCUS ON PERSONS

Those who seek to bring peace in legal conflict must deal with real issues of alleged fact, liability, duty, and justice. They will have to help the parties resolve their dispute. But since there is a commitment to the biblical call for reconciliation, the people involved in the dispute are often as important as the dispute itself. What is happening to the persons involved? What attitudes are developing? How is the dispute affecting their spiritual vitality? Their health?

In the class meetings of early Methodism each participant was asked, "How is it going with your soul?" In our day of specialization there are people who inquire about our taxes, our bank balances, our pulse rate, our IRA accounts, our credit ratings. But who really asks, "How is it going with your soul?" It would be a terrible mistake not to consider the person's guilts, fears, and lostness. Reconciliation and peace are essentially about people who have disputes, not about disputes people have.

This is one reason that the church's involvement in legal peacemaking can become such a powerful healing ministry. People in legal conflict are often caught up in crisis: injury, financial loss, loss of family and friends, business failure, or pride and ego damage. Many are very vulnerable. How tragic that at such times we often become mere technicians—persons with skill and information, but without spiritual capacity. Hurting people are often directed to those who channel the anxiety and loss into destructive patterns.

Peacemakers and reconcilers must be available to provide healing, not only in the relationship, but within the persons themselves. We seek whole and peace-full persons, for they can develop healed and vital relationships and use times of conflict as opportunities for personal and relational growth. To resolve issues but leave persons essentially unchanged—unforgiving, isolated, unaware of the peace of Christ—is not an adequate mission for Christian peacemakers.

To focus on Jesus is not a mere act of piety, but takes seriously the example Christ set for believers. Jesus not only taught a way to find reconciliation and peace, he demonstrated it. As John tells us, "The Word became flesh and dwelt among us."

In Philippians 2:5-11 Paul describes how Christ emptied himself and refused to claim his full rights and privileges. He spurned power and glory and chose the cross in order to be a reconciler.

Jesus teaches and demonstrates a new perspective on victory, rights, and power. In his temptation he rejected the use of power and miracles to create the kingdom. He rejected the sword when Peter tried to protect him in the Garden of Gethsemane, and he remained silent when Pilate urged him to defend himself.

This one who, with his supernatural attributes could have silenced opponents and shattered their defenses with his intellect, rejected all of that for a way of lowliness. He won the victory as a suffering servant, a slain lamb.

Jesus listened to those who asked for help; he refused to be judgmental. He gathered the wounded and hurting to himself, and broke through the rules and traditions that brought division and disunity.

Jesus was not some mere passive mediator. He did not merely try to bring God and man together and invite them to work out some agreement. Nor was he merely a clever counselor, able to invite discussion, draw people out with Rogerian skills, surface emotional tensions, and suggest compromises. Perhaps he did all of those things, but he was also an involved and participating mediator. He had a stake in the reconciling process. He was not a casual observer, a

FOCUS ON THE EXAMPLE OF JESUS

hired professional. He gave his life on the cross so that healing might take place.

The mediator who is simply an effective counselor does an important, even noble task. But a mediator in the fullest biblical context is not a disinterested third party. He is one of the parties himself. His love for the disputants and his concern for the wholeness of the church will drive the Christian mediator to an agonizing, praying, and giving type of mediation. Often the impasse is shattered and broken by the mediator's acting in love amidst the parties' anger and alienation.

At a point of impasse in a dispute between a building contractor and a local church about cost overruns and contract provisions, the mediator asked the contractor the price of his air flight to the mediation setting. He then wrote a check for that amount and gave it to the contractor, indicating he wanted to invest in reconciliation. The act triggered a series of exchanges, which totally reversed the defensiveness and alienation that had characterized the discussions. It was not an act of technique and timing, not a clever ruse, but a spontaneous gift that showed the mediator's deep desire to see the dispute resolved.

On other occasions mediators have made loans, offered housing, arranged work opportunities, and spent hours in prayer—expressing commitments to healing and reconciliation.

There is a vulnerability in Jesus' giving and living, a risking, an openness that is shocking to modern man, tutored as he is in insurance policies, defensive legal structures, and carefully chosen words. We have forgotten how to be vulnerable by confessing our problems and inadequacies and by giving unqualified love to others. Instead, we protect ourselves and talk of controlling "downside risks."

Have you ever noticed a settlement agreement drafted by lawyers? The language is full of denials: "So-and so, denying any liability whatsoever and denying all allegations of so-and-so, nevertheless, in order to promote a settlement, makes a voluntary gift of $2,500 in return for which so-and-so waives any and all claims." Don't risk honesty. Protect. Defend!

How contrary to the whole mission and life of Christ, who died for his vulnerability. Perhaps mediators shall, on occasion, suffer and be blamed by those who refuse their reconciling love—shall even, perhaps, be sued! But even then, those whom Christ calls to obedience and discipleship will see mediation as a worthwhile ministry of love.

FOCUS ON THE SPIRIT

The conviction that resolution takes place in a spiritual realm is central to the believer's capacity to minister in human conflict. This dimension totally transforms one's understanding of the process. When we view a conflict as part of the larger spiritual reality of this world, it helps put it into proper perspective. It helps us see that we are not dealing merely with some human quarrel, but that this dispute is in some sense a part of the larger disunity of the cosmos, the alienation and separation that Jesus came to overcome by his church. In fact, Paul tells us that the very rocks are crying out, eager for everything to come into unity in Christ. When I minister for peace and reconciliation I am participating in the call of God and the creation of his will.

MIRACLE AND MYSTERY

Recognizing the Spirit's presence gives the reconciler an openness to miracle and mystery—the invasion of lives by the grace of God. Without such an openness, there would often be despair and hopelessness in the face of the complex, seemingly intractable conflicts that need reconciliation.

How often we restrict the capacity of the Spirit to break through barriers. We have eyes that cannot see, spirits that cannot hope. We too easily accept stones when Christ wishes to provide fish, or even a banquet. Who would have given much chance that an old, first-century Jew like Peter would rejoice and fellowship with a gentile? Impossible would have been the human verdict. A few might have ventured to suggest that maybe someday, but not now. Too early. Too difficult!

After all, we are not the reconcilers; Jesus is. Many times a team of mediators has met and shared their despair at a particularly intractable dispute, one built on years of "injustice collecting." They have often begun the proceedings by stating, "There is no human solution, no clever technique learned in training programs. Only the potential of inviting Jesus Christ into the dispute as the reconciler can break through the anger."

HOPE AND PATIENCE

How easy it is to succumb to our own agendas, which demand immediate solutions. We want to see the growing fruit of peace now. We want to sow, water, and reap. But if we minister as legal peacemakers in the context of the Spirit, we can learn to wait—and do so with hope. We can "fail," "lose," be "unsuccessful," and yet commit it to our Lord. After all, we are seeking to be used in his time and his way. The Spirit of Christ will tend the gift we leave. When we release ourselves from the need for a "success" or a "victory," we receive real power for service.

So often we have seen the necessity of hope and patience in domestic conflict. Often we have felt God's healing provision, but it has seemed to be unaccepted. Yet, the many cases where couples have been reunited after divorce have been triumphs of watered seeds. What triumphant celebrations those remarriages have been!

JUSTICE

We are told by Paul to "speak the truth in love," an almsot impossible task. We all know both vigorous, brutal "truthtellers" and those supposed lovers who are always sweet and tender. But those who wish to be legal peacemakers must seek truth and justice. Without such a commitment it is too easy, in the words of the prophet Jeremiah (6:14), to say "Peace, peace; when there is no peace." It is too easy to avoid real substantive issues by smothering them with false spirituality. A commitment to justice may involve confrontation and struggle. A commitment to justice means that wrong and sin may need to be acknowledged and confessed to enable restoration and restitution to take place.

On rare occasions legal peacemakers may have to call persons to account for their behavior. After all, Paul confronted Peter about his conduct (Gal. 2:11).

In one case that came before the CCS, the mediating team discovered that a pattern of unethical business conduct had followed one of the parties throughout several businesses. The task of the mediators was not simply to reconcile these persons—nor just to restore the improperly taken funds—but to call the believer to account for his manner of doing business and invite him to repent. Such confrontation by mediators/arbitrators is rare. But it is part of what the church is called to do. The sinner must be given a chance for real restoration and peace.

G. H. C. McGregor, commenting on Matthew 18, noted, "Here we have the first hint of the truth (that) . . . justice is truly vindicated, not when the wrongdoer is compelled to make reparation, but when the unjust will is 'won' to justice."

FORGIVENESS

Forgiveness is painful! Forgiveness can be an escape! Forgiveness is the command of Christ!

Forgiveness has become all of these things because the word *forgiveness* has been used so loosely. What does it really mean? When can it be a liberating, empowering experience? When is it illusory, falsely humble, a producer of bitterness and alienation?

The Bible calls us to forgiveness in the middle of our conflicts. Following the section of Matthew 18 that we looked at earlier, Jesus tells a parable about forgiveness.

A poor servant, unable to repay a huge debt to his king, has the whole debt forgiven when he pleads for mercy. Soon after, this same man throws a fellow servant in prison for nonpayment of a minor sum. When the king hears of this, he is furious, recalls the previously forgiven servant, and has him committed to prison. The unforgiving servant lost the grace he had received. "If you forgive other people their failures, your Heavenly Father will also forgive you. But if you will not forgive . . . neither will your Father forgive you your failures" (Matt. 6:14, Phillips).

It is quite clear that many persons with le-

gal conflicts are filled with a spirit of unforgiveness. They are unwilling to let the
slightest wrong go by without demanding
"justice." They refuse to release the resentment they have. Many who come to CCS
want the peace of Christ—may even want
the dispute resolved—but they still nurture
the wrong they feel. They refuse to display
the love, generosity, unselfishness, and
sacrifice of Christ. They derive a degree of
sympathy and satisfaction from retaining a
grudge and feeling sorry for themselves.
Like the man by the pool of Bethesda, it is
not at all clear that they want to be healed.

No conciliation ministry that emerges from
a Christian commitment can avoid the invitation to give and receive forgiveness. Our
own capacity to forgive is directly related to
our apprehension and appropriation of God's
forgiveness of ourselves. And our capacity to
receive forgiveness from God is related to
our capacity to forgive others.

Frequently in dealing with people in legal
conflict there are profound issues where forgiveness is sometimes the only healing remedy. Perhaps the party at fault has no
money to pay for damages, or perhaps the
wrong simply cannot be compensated for
with money. What can the libeler offer?
Confession and a request for forgiveness is
the most powerful reparation. Even where
money is repaid or damages compensated,
there is still the need to release the anger or
bitterness, the guilt and alienation so often
present.

But biblical forgiveness is not avoidance of
the conflict. It is not saying "forget it" to the
guilty party. It is not flight from encounter.
It is not pretending that wrong has not been
done. Often Christians mistake forgiveness
for avoiding the conflict and internalizing

the anger and bitterness, which results in resentment toward others, anger at the world and at life, and medical and psychological problems.

Real forgiveness takes the conflict quite seriously, recognizing that confession and forgiveness are a process completed only in relation to others. We cannot forgive all by ourselves without actually offering that forgiveness to the other person. How often we want forgiveness, but will not directly ask to be forgiven.

A Christian building contractor asked CCS to arbitrate a dispute with an employee. The employer had made a substantial loan to the employee for the down payment on a house. Some time later when the debt was to be repaid, the employee told the employer that he was not going to repay the loan. God had told him not to. At first the employer felt a natural anger and a strong sense that the young man should not be allowed to use God as an excuse for his own failure. The employer fired the young man and called on CCS to arbitrate the issue of the debt.

As the mediator spoke with the employer, the option of forgiveness was raised. Forgive? In a case like this? What a precedent! The employee was a sinner, a thief, a fraud! Surely God could not be indicating that option. But after a few days of prayer the employer felt a strong leading from the Lord to forego the debt and forgive the employee. He went to the employee and offered him forgiveness. Later he even gave him his job back—at a higher wage. Less than a year later the employee was the chief instrument of healing in the employer's marriage.

Most of us are willing to forgive if the other party restores the damage and is appropriately penitent. To forgive first—to act as

Christ did, who loved us while we were yet sinners—is shocking! Only people who know the reality beyond this world can understand this way of thinking.

7 RECONCILING COVENANTS

"Guilty!" "Fifteen thousand dollars plus costs for the plaintiff." "Complaint dismissed." These are typical judgments of the courts. They are attempts to redress wrongs. In legal language, the court provides "remedies" for wrongs.

There is, in fact, a legal maxim: "For every wrong there is a remedy." It expresses the conviction that there is a means of redressing any legal wrong. But that is not really true at all. There are a host of wrongs, a great number of harms, for which the legal system offers no real remedy. Is there really a remedy for an insult, other than an apology? How about a remedy for hate? For silent treatments? For refusals to care? So often people try to quantify their hurt.

Recently a number of Japanese-Americans sought reparation from the U.S. government for interning Japanese-Americans during the Second World War. They demanded $3 billion. Was that equivalent to their loss of property and freedom? Or what of some of the Iranian hostages who wanted the U.S. government to pay $1,000 a day for the time they were held captive? The presidential commission suggested $12.50 per day. Was either equal to the suffering and anguish? Was either really a "remedy"?

The courts are severely limited in the remedies they can provide for wrongs. In fact most legal remedies are money judgments. In some circumstances courts may require one to honor a contract, award custody of a child, or issue an injunction preventing further wrong. But these nonmonetary judgments are quite limited. Most often, compensation and redress are measured in dollars.

If I punch you, you may sue me. The punch cannot, of course, be withdrawn, and the court will not authorize a return blow. It might, however, require me to pay your medical bills and provide money as compensation for your pain and suffering. But it is helpless to deal with my hate, my envy, my jealousy.

If I have libeled you (broken our relationship, shattered friendships and covenants), the courts can do little about that except transfer money. They can't touch my desire to destroy you. Tom Harris's suit of the pastor for $19.5 million for alleging that Harris had committed suicide is illustrative. The pastor has apologized, asked forgiveness, retracted his statement. But the legal system pays little attention to these real remedies. It will simply decide how many dollars are owed to Harris. Certainly dollars do little to foster reconciliation. They may be appropriate where restitution is essential or where one's wrong has created monetary losses, but certainly dollars don't heal wounds, cleanse memories, or foster love.

Viewed from the perspective of a concern for restoring relationships money is not only inadequate, it may even serve as a further barrier, a last impediment or insult. Surely there must be better alternatives, more imaginative options for those charged by Scripture with acting as mediators and arbitrators in disputes among believers.

Creative, restorative, and redemptive remedies are needed. Christians who serve as legal peacemakers must not be trapped by secular court models of redress and remedies. To be sure, restitution is a sound biblical principle. But Christian mediators must go beyond mere recompense, beyond penalties, even, where possible, beyond justice. The commitment of Scripture is not only the resolution of the dispute, but the reconciliation of the parties.

A recent case in a western state dramatically illustrates this concern. Two Christian families who lived next door to each other had their relationship clouded for years with numerous civil and even criminal complaints against each other. They fought over property lines, over unsightly trash in one of the family's yards. They forbade their children to play with each other. Finally, a confrontation occurred in which the husband of one couple struck the other's wife, and a lawsuit was instituted. When the CCS mediator met with the couples, he was uncertain how to begin, recognizing this as a conflict that grew out of deep hostility and bitterness. He invited the couples to pray with him that God might heal, restore, and break through years of hostilities even as he broke down walls between gentiles and Jews to make one new people in Christ.

In what the mediator later described as little short of a miracle, the couples were confessing to each other and developing solutions to their disputes only two hours later. What is critical to note, however, is the character of the agreement reached. Money certainly was not the issue. Nor was the concern simply to stop the bickering and violence. The goal was to put these couples in the path of reconciliation where real healing and restoration could occur.

The agreement resolved some factual issues, but also created some covenants to rebuild relationships and chart specific steps to encourage sharing and understanding. For example, the agreement included a yard-cleaning day with both parties involved, and the mediator participating, too. The parties agreed to weekly dinners together for a defined period of time to provide common play opportunities for their children.

In another case, an elderly lady complained that the continued late evening activities of a student who rented an apartment above her set her dog to barking all night, preventing any sleep. The mediators worked out some shared meals between the student and lady so that the dog got to know the student and stopped his barking. The young man got some good, home-cooked meals to boot!

These kinds of remedies—commitments to spend time together, to worship together, to support each other—are precisely what the church needs to call persons to make and keep. Though in most cases a court could not enforce such remedies, nor could an arbitrator require them, they answer not only the legal issues but encourage reconciliation.

Anthropological studies of primitive legal systems reveal such relationship-centered remedies. The priest/judge of a tribe faced with a dispute over who killed a tribal member's pig would not only decide who must pay whom for the pig; he might also require a festival where both parties brought food and provided entertainment. The festival would be structured to conclude the dispute and move the relationship back into a positive direction.

Biblical tradition is also replete with the concept of covenant—binding agreements between parties who willingly commit themselves to live together in certain ways with mutual obligations. The covenant may be a legally binding agreement. But it is more than that; it establishes a relationship. The covenanters are bound by promise, by family, and by community.

Christians need to rediscover the power of covenanting with each other—sealing relationships, committing themselves to each other and to structures that nurture their lives. Not every issue mediated or arbitrated will require elaborate covenants or specially creative remedies. But to the extent the disputes have breached the relationship or divided the body, such models might well be considered.

Covenants might include agreements to review the relationship at some specified future date, to share in some ministry together, and to pray regularly for each other. The disputants might participate in a worship service, thanking God for his reconciling intervention, or enroll themselves in a mediator-training program. Some of these remedies will be substantive—that is, they will address the specific problem. Others, such as signing covenants or sharing in worship experiences, will be testimonial and symbolic of their commitments. The concept of covenant offers Christian mediators and arbitrators a powerful tool in framing remedies and making commitments that can move us toward the sort of relationships God calls us to.

While the area of remedies illustrates that aspects of biblical mediation and arbitration go substantially beyond the provisions of the law, the essential elements of this ministry are not only "legal" but have received strong endorsements from state legislators and bar associations. The legal system encourages precisely such procedures.

Mr. David Brink, president of the American Bar Association in 1981, called the creation of alternate systems to traditional courts a "boon to lawyers. They will be seen as counselors, problem solvers, and deliverers of prompt, appropriate, and affordable justice."

From the popular writers to Chief Justice Warren Burger, there is a widespread recognition of the inability of our legal system to deal with the multitude of wrongs that occur in a society as large, depersonalized, and complex as ours. Chief Justice Burger has been particularly concerned with the need for alternatives to formal litigation. "We need to consider adopting neighborhood-type dispute mechanisms, used by both underdeveloped and very advanced societies. By whatever name we call it—arbitration, mediation, conciliation, or a combination of all three—centuries of human experience undergirds these informal kinds of procedures."

As long ago as 1976 the American Bar Association's National Conference on the Causes of Popular Dissatisfaction with the Administration of Justice considered suggestions that justice could be better served by "processes less time-consuming and less expensive" and that "nonjudicial tribunals utilizing nonlawyers be considered."

And in 1977 the ABA Report of the National Conference on Minor Dispute Resolution noted that in a typical dispute between

LEGAL DIMENSIONS OF CHRISTIAN CONCILIATION

neighbors, often "court action is unlikely to address the basic underlying issues. What is at the root of the continuing conflict between these individuals? How can they be helped to get along better in the future?"

After noting the quickening pace of modern life, the waning of traditional dispute resolution institutions such as the family, the church, and the neighborhood, the report went on: "But perhaps the problem goes deeper. Along with the frustration engendered by the unresponsiveness of the legal system, there has come a perceptible disenchantment with the increasing complexity and remoteness of the traditional dispute resolution process. . . . Disputants appear to yearn for a simple and accessible procedure that permits them to tell their story and get prompt and constructive assistance. . . ."

Increasingly the leadership of the American Bar Association has encouraged the creation of a variety of alternatives to court systems. The American Arbitration Association has prompted mediation and arbitration programs throughout the United States, providing training and professional leadership especially in labor and commercial disputes. Diversion programs, community dispute resolution centers, neighborhood justice centers, and legal aid clinics are just a few of the structures that have been encouraged. Such alternatives do not challenge the legal system; they respond to the system's own plea for forms of justice that meet personal and community needs in prompt, economical, and just ways.

THE LAW AND MEDIATION/ ARBITRATION   Laws in virtually every state encourage arbitration and mediation as a means of resolving disputes. Many of these laws are patterned after, or at least reflect, the basic elements of the Uniform Arbitration Act approved by the American Bar Association in 1955 and 1956. That act (which has no force but is only a model) provides that written agreements to submit present or future controversies to arbitration are "valid, enforceable, and irrevocable." The Act establishes procedures for enforcing such agreements, the appointment of arbitrators, conduct of hearings, the role of witnesses and powers of arbitrators, and matters relating to review of arbitrator awards by the courts. (See Appendix 1 for the full text of the Uniform Arbitration Act.)

Statutes not only permit such processes, but, in certain states, mediation or advisory arbitration is required in suits involving claims under a certain amount of money. For example, a California statute requires that disputes under $15,000 be submitted to a mediation service before the matter may be tried in the civil courts.

Arbitration has become a primary means of resolving disputes in labor contracts and in certain commercial disputes. Many union contracts contain clauses that require that any dispute about the contract be arbitrated. Such clauses, which are advance agreements to submit to arbitration, have been upheld by the courts and specifically provided for in the Uniform Arbitration Act.

The law affects mediation and arbitration in a number of specific ways. First, the law provides for, and will enforce, advance agreements to arbitrate disputes regarding a contract or other legal matter. Second, a settlement reached during mediation will generally be enforced by the courts if that settlement reflects an agreement of the parties to solve the dispute in a specific way. The court enforces such settlements because they represent a contract between the parties.

Third, the law encourages mediation procedures by providing that statements made in such sessions may not be used in court if the mediation sessions fail. Fourth, the courts will enforce the decision of an arbitrator(s) whom the parties have agreed on and given power to decide between them. This is based primarily on contract law; the courts will protect the rights of parties under a contract. If the parties have agreed to submit an issue to an arbitrator, the court will enforce the decision arrived at under that process.

Since arbitration is a contractual process, the agreement between the parties, usually referred to as the submission agreement, is vital in determining the scope of the arbitrator's authority. This submission agreement signals the intent of the parties to submit a specific issue or set of issues to arbitration and usually indicates something of the process and persons who will be involved. The more precise the arbitration agreement, the less likely the agreement can be challenged in court for vagueness or uninformed consent.

Often rather than spelling out all the details of how arbitrators might be selected and other questions, certain rules of procedure are incorporated into a submission agreement by a general clause, which indicates that the matter presently in dispute (or alternatively, disputes arising out of a given contract) shall be submitted to arbitration under the rules and procedures of the American Arbitration Association or it could say the Christian Conciliation Service or the Mennonite Conciliation Service. (See appendices for a sample of such a clause.)

The rights of parties not included in the

arbitration are not affected by the agreement between the arbitrating parties. Two parties may not agree on issues that affect the rights of another person to a contract. Similarly, courts will carefully review mediated or arbitrated solutions to child-custody matters since the child is usually not a participant; the state has an interest in protecting the unrepresented child.

In many ways the arbitrator has more power than a judge. A judge is bound by decisions (precedents) in previous cases, and his decisions are reviewed by higher courts. Arbitrators have much more flexibility. Their decisions may be reviewed by higher courts only on very narrow grounds, such as evidence the arbitrator was not impartial (he was a close friend of one of the parties but withheld that information) or his decision exceeded the powers given to him by the arbitration agreement.

Thus the ministry of conciliation within the church is a legitimate response to the needs of our entire judicial system—one encouraged by the professional bar associations and by the law.

8

HISTORICAL PRECEDENTS

The development of a distinctively Christian alternative for the resolution of disputes between believers may seem novel and peculiar. However, a study of history and other cultures reveals that the development of alternative legal systems is quite common. If a subculture has a strong sense of identity and group values that seem different from the prevailing culture, the subculture is often reluctant to relegate responsibility for resolving members' disputes to those whose values and beliefs are alien to their own. For example, in the early days of the Mormons' settlement of Utah, they established conciliation courts and condemned members' use of civil courts to resolve disputes.

In many nations that have a diversity of cultural and religious subgroups, a variety of court systems have coexisted, allowing the different communities to use courts that reflect their own values, culturally and legally. Communities with strong, religious character frequently involve the religious leadership in resolving disputes.

On the Bahamian island of Mayaguana, cases appear before church elders either because the principals have asked for their intervention or because someone in the community has alerted them to the dispute. The council will ask the parties to appear at the church—or other convenient location—and each party will state his side of the dispute, presenting witnesses and cross-examining if appropriate. The council elicits facts, questions witnesses, and as an anthropologist describes it "is concerned with the wider implications of the charges . . . seeking to determine the source of the tensions."[1]

Virtually all cases are solved by the council, which acts primarily as a mediator, suggesting ways of resolving the tensions and, if necessary, assigning the minister to act as a personal mediator. Major efforts are made to reconcile the disputants. After the resolution of a dispute, the council continues to monitor the relationship to assure that a flare-up does not occur. "The church uses familiar jargon and adjudicates cases in a very relaxed fashion," the anthropologist writes.

"There is no effort on its part to find one party guilty and the other innocent; it is generally assumed that the disputants are more concerned with reconciliation and conflict settlement than they are with retribution."

THE JEWISH EXPERIENCE

In 1968, Black and Puerto Rican tenants living in a deteriorating section of Boston took their landlords to court. They complained that the buildings were rat-infested and unsafe and accused the landlords of rent gouging. The landlords countered that the tenants failed to pay rents as agreed, and that the problems were a result of tenant misconduct, including the willful destruction of property. An arbitration panel was established which, after hearings and negotiations, found both sides at fault. Both parties were asked to sign an agreement listing their rights and responsibilities. The landlords were committed to proper janitorial service, new locks to provide safe quarters, periodic painting of the premises, and adequate utilities. The tenants had to take responsibility for their own premises for the damage caused by their guests.

The court that decided this case was not a United States district court nor a court of the State of Massachusetts, but a rabbinical court, a Jewish judicial body with a history that dates back to biblical times. Jewish courts *(bet din)* go back to the time of Moses and Jethro (Exodus 19). Variations evolved in the pre-Christian era.

The Jewish experience is relevant because its commitments are also rooted in Scripture with God's character (just, righteous, and merciful) forming the foundation for law. The Jewish community, like the Christian, has a profound sense of the uniqueness of God's revelation and its claim upon all our lives in both personal and corporate dimensions.

The long experience of Jews as a minority people, often as a captive people, has taught them to preserve values and processes that encode their commitments to justice and God's commandments. They have preserved their judicial autonomy from the time of the Babylonian exile. As one historian noted, "Just as the essence and continuity of the religious life . . . was not affected by the people going into exile, so also the legal life—the commandments pertaining to man's relationships with his fellow man, such as property law, contracts, torts, parts of criminal law . . . and so on, continued to subsist and evolve."[2] These judicial entities found their meaning and source in the Torah (the first five books of the Old Testament) and the teachings of the rabbis.

The captors and political rulers of the Jews usually allowed them to maintain their own judicial systems. In fifteenth-century Spain, for example, a conference of communal representatives drew up *takkonot* (ordinances): widespread codifications of their legal and administrative systems. The introduction illustrates the basis of the Jewish legal autonomy:

Since it is the desire and merciful will of our Lord, the King . . . that civil and criminal cases be tried under the laws of the Jews, and he has commanded in his charter of privileges that the honorable Don Abraham, whom God protects, shall try such cases, he and the judges whom he may appoint in his place, wherefrom great benefits will accrue to the communities: first, the Jews will thereby observe their Torah; second, they will free themselves of the many costs and losses that they incur when they resort to the gentile courts; third, although they are very learned and rightful and just men, the (gentile) judges are not familiar with our laws and statutes . . . and moreover, since our Lord the King, whom God saves, has in his said charter commanded his judges and magistrates not to interfere in litigation between one Jew and another.[3]

So extensive was the Jewish commitment to their own law and judicial administration that soon after the destruction of the temple in A.D. 70, when Roman imperial rule temporarily restricted their judicial autonomy, the Talmud *(Tanhumah Mishpatim,* portion 6) declared:

Rabbi Tarfon used to say: Wherever you find gentile agora (law courts), even though their law is the same as the law of Israel, you may not resort to them.

This rejection of gentile courts, even when their substantive law was the same, became a governing decision. Jews were not to use the gentile courts in disputes among themselves. Resort to a gentile court was equated with a denial of the divine presence and the Torah. It constituted a profanation of the name of God. Maimonides, the twelfth-century Talmudic authority, noted the conclusion: "Whoever litigates according to gentile law and in their courts, although their laws are the same as the laws of Israel, is an evildoer and he is deemed to have reviled and blasphemed and rebelled against the Torah of Moses our Teacher." Use of gentile courts made one an "informer." In 1150 the rabbinical council at Troyes decreed excommunication for offenders.

This commitment was the major factor in preserving the Jewish courts. These institutions included not only rabbinical courts, presided over by official judges, but arbitration courts and lay tribunals in various forms. In fact, the first lay arbitration panels date to the second century when the official Jewish courts were overthrown following the revolt of Bar Kochba. Even after the reinstitution of the rabbinical courts, the lay institutions survived.

In the Middle Ages, the *bet din* heard all types of cases: religious, civil, and criminal. In religious and ritual matters, Talmudic law was strictly followed, but in civil matters, the courts sought to harmonize the law of the land with Jewish law, unless this law was thought to be totally unjust (such as laws discriminating against Jews).

Most criminal matters during this time were heard by government courts. The Jewish courts had little authority except in the case of "informers," who were punishable by excommunication, fine, or, in extreme cases, capital punishment. In minor criminal matters the *bet din* did exercise authority: dishonesty in business dealings, desertion, wife beating, and other social and ethical violations. A complaint was issued by one party and then a court summons to the other party. Failure to appear could result in a lien on property or excommunication. Each party pleaded their own cause without lawyers, and the hearings were held promptly.

Many Jewish courts continue to function throughout the world including the United States. Their authority varies widely from country to country. In the United States the largest and most established is the Bet Din of the Rabbinical Council of America, a body associated with the Orthodox Jewish community. It deals primarily with religious matters of divorce, marriage, and excommunication. The matters it handles are generally not adversarial in nature.

Both religious and business disputes are heard by other established rabbinical courts, such as those in New York City. The Orthodox German community has a court that functions with a three-judge panel of rabbis. For business disputes the parties must sign a submission agreement. Procedures are informal and lawyers are present only when requested by one of the parties. Records are destroyed after the hearings to insure confidentiality; however, the decision is made in writing. If one of the parties refuses to abide by the decision, the panel may allow the other party to take the decision to the civil court for enforcement.

In addition to the rabbinical courts, there are a number of Jewish arbitration and conciliation boards. One of the best known is the Jewish Conciliation Board of New York City, established in the 1920s. It currently handles close to one thousand cases annually, including a substantial proportion of family and domestic matters. Most cases before the board are settled prior to formal trial, which only occurs 8½ percent of the time.

The complaining party brings the matter to the executive secretary of the board, who decides if the action should proceed. If so, the party fills out a complaint form, a copy of which is sent to the other party, requesting that they come and explain their side. Follow-up letters and the moral persuasion of the community are the only pressures that encourage compliance, which is very common.

In many cases the matter is resolved during mediation sessions with the executive secretary. If not, both parties complete a signed submission form and the matter is docketed for a hearing before the board, which consists of three judges: a rabbi, a businessman, and a lawyer chosen by the executive secretary. Proceedings are informal, with both sides telling their story and the judges questioning witnesses. The judges then issue a written opinion, which is kept on record with the transcript of the trial.

The primary basis used by the judges in deciding cases is referred to as *mishpat shalom* (judgment of peace), a process that focuses on reconciliation without adjudication of fault or blame. *Mishpat shalom* tends to be a combination of Jewish law and common sense. The process often ends with the parties kissing. Said one commentator, "We are not attempting to say who is morally or legally justified, we are trying to reconcile the relationship. . . . There must be compassion and forgiveness."

Of course, it was not only special judicial systems that reflected the application of religious principles. The development of English common law, which is the basis of American law, involved religious concepts and principles and a substantial number of the clergy. There are striking and extensive parallels between English substantive and procedural law and biblical principles and rules. It is quite clear that the English Christian heritage shaped the common law. John Warwick Montgomery has detailed many of these parallels in his volume *Law and Gospel: A Study in Jurisprudence.* One especially interesting element of English legal history is the development of the Courts of Equity.

As the legal system of England became unified and "common," Roman and Canon (church) law were shaping forces. Many of the royal judges were clerics, both because they were among the few educated persons and for economy since they had incomes from their clerical positions. During the thirteenth and fourteenth centuries, however, a body of professional lawyers developed. By 1300 most English lawyers were trained in the Inns of Court. These lawyers were less influenced by Canon law and far fewer of them were clergy.

The royal courts and the law also became increasingly rigid and inflexible during this period. The rules, which covered the common law, became highly technical and artificial. Many legal problems emerged that the "law" simply failed to address at all. In other cases the insistence on the "letter of the law" often produced injustice.

Increasingly, persons whose claims were not addressed by the law courts appealed to the king who had a duty as a Christian to justice beyond the dictates of the law. The king had, in fact, extraordinary powers as the "fountain of justice." Over a period of time it became customary for petitions to the king to be directed to the chancellor, a counselor to the king, who was the "keeper of the king's conscience." The chancellor was also a leading church official (Sir Thomas More was perhaps the most famous).

These appeals for justice originally occurred primarily in areas where the common law provided no rules or legal structures, but increasingly appeals were made where the royal courts, applying the common law with rigidity, produced results that seemed contrary to justice.

If a party failed to deliver a payment for land he was buying on the date required, strict performance of the contract would call for him to forfeit the land, even though he had made many payments and was prepared to bring the payments up-to-date (including interest for the period of delay). The common-law courts might be unmoved by the debtor's plea and order the land returned to the mortgage holder. But when the debtor went to the chancellor, he might prevail—not on the basis of the law, but on the basis of justice, or what was called equity.

Thus, there gradually developed an "equity" court ruled over by the chancellor, a court also called the Court of Chancery. These courts, administered in the early period by clerics, had a strong religious flavor, both because of the chancellor's role and the moral rules that governed the process. Decisions were made not on the basis of the abstract principles of the law, but on the basis of what seemed right, just, and equitable.

For example, "rules" of equity were: "He who seeks equity, must do equity" and "He who comes into equity must come with clean hands." These maxims expressed the notion that ethical factors were relevant to the decisions of the equity court. One could not seek the moral support of the court unless one was willing to do "right" and had conducted oneself properly in regard to the issue at hand. The key element was "conscience"—the application of what was "right." The chancellor's power was one of "conscience," and his appeal to the parties was over "conscience." In fact, when the "law" and the chancellor clashed, the chancellor did not overrule or abolish the law, but simply indicated that the parties could not, because of "conscience," enforce an unjust decision. Based on such considerations, equity courts often clashed with the common-law courts.

Eventually the equity courts ceased to be the province of the clergy, and, after Sir Thomas More, chancellors were increasingly laymen. The equity court continued, however, to be a separate structure with its own principles and rules until the late nineteenth century in England. The courts of law and equity were also transplanted into the American legal system. In virtually all of our states today, the courts of law and equity have merged into a single system. Still, some of the distinctions that marked the earlier division continue to affect the legal system today.

What is especially worth noting in our context, however, is not simply the involvement of the clergy in the equity court, but the recognition that justice and equity relate to ethical and moral principles, which are largely derived from religious traditions, and that such values may at times run counter to the demands of "law." Conscience may require more than law, or even something distinct from law.

The emergence of such systems in four-teenth-century England constitutes a warning to the legal structures of our own day not to become so rigid and rule bound that they cease to do justice, nor foreclose the possibility that at times the "law" may be an instrument of injustice—a point that created controversy between Jesus and the Pharisees. The experience of medieval England—however different the social and legal context—also suggests that the church may apply its commitments to equity and justice, and at times command through the conscience of its people solutions that are distinct from those of the law.

PART 4

PEACEMAKING GIFTS

9 PROCESSES FOR CONCILIATION

How are the concepts of Christian conciliation actually applied? What happens in mediation and arbitration? While there is a considerable flexibility in both a legal and spiritual sense, the Christian Conciliation Service has developed some general procedures, which parties follow when they have a dispute.

COMMUNICATING THE BIBLICAL CONCILIATION ALTERNATIVE

Since the entire process of mediation or arbitration requires the parties' consent, the first step in Christian conciliation is to suggest the mediation or arbitration option. Many cases come to us through referrals by pastors, lawyers, and counselors. Often, however, the contact is made directly by one of the parties who wishes to explore the possibility of conciliation. Some information may be sent to the disputants by mail, but often their willingness to consider this option depends on the encouragement of a neutral third party such as the pastor, counselor, or lawyer.

Sometimes it is difficult to get parties to consider conciliation as an alternative to their natural tendency to initiate a lawsuit.

They have legitimate uncertainties about what the conciliation process will entail and what its outcome might be. Other times they think they have a good "case," so why take the risk of some novel and strange proceeding. Too often we have encountered Christian organizations, even ministry groups, whose conviction that they have a solid legal claim causes them to reject the risks of conciliation.

The parties' attorneys may also resist the use of these biblical procedures. This resistance may come from their lack of spiritual perspective, a lack of confidence in the quality of the program, or a belief that such a process would not be in the best interests of their client.

Occasionally parties have a curious objection to arbitration. A church involved in a bitter, congregational split was challenged to consider arbitration. One faction agreed but the other declined, indicating they didn't want someone "deciding for them." Of course, since suits had already been filed, the question was not whether someone was going to decide, but rather who would make the decision, when the decision would be made, with what process, and from what perspectives. Until the Christian community recognizes the biblical commission that underlies conciliation, there will be resistance to this process.

An effective means of suggesting mediation or arbitration is to get both parties to participate in an informal session at which the philosophy and purposes of conciliation may be explained. Occasionally, the parties will know enough about the program and principles to agree to mediation or arbitration without an exploratory meeting. But often

A PRELIMINARY MEETING

such a session is necessary and the following points can be explained:

- The biblical teaching about reconciliation and the procedures indicated in Matthew 18 and 1 Corinthians 6.
- The fact that conciliation involves a concern for both the legal issues and the emotional and spiritual health of the individuals involved and their relationship to one another.
- The legal consequences of agreeing to mediation or arbitration.
- The distinction between mediation, arbitration, and med/arb.
- Any costs involved in the process. (CCS normally charges a fifty-dollar fee for those who utilize the service, but there is no charge for the mediators, unless the matter becomes substantially prolonged.)
- The advantages of the conciliation process, which is biblically faithful, focuses on relationships, is more informal, and less costly. The parties will share in the process by selecting the mediators or arbitrators and defining the issues. Generally the resolution is speedy and results in a worthwhile witness to the world.

At this meeting the parties and their counsel (lawyers, friends, pastors), if they are present, are encouraged to raise questions so they truly understand the conciliation process. Then they must decide whether or not they wish to proceed. If so, various decisions must be made (either as a part of this session or later).

The role of the parties in making these decisions should not be underestimated. One of the reasons processes such as mediation and arbitration have had such a successful rate of settlement is the participation of the parties in the resolution process. In a litigation setting, parties rarely feel they "own" the process. It is rather something the state imposes on them. They are strapped by extensive procedural rules. They don't pick the time, the place, or the judge. They may even feel they never really had the chance to tell their story. They rarely feel they have received a fair hearing—what a lawyer is likely to call "due process." The very opportunity for the disputants to make decisions about the process creates a different atmosphere.

SELECTING THE PROCESS   Sometime during this preliminary meeting or shortly thereafter, the parties must select mediation, arbitration, or mediation/arbitration. Whatever process is selected, it is helpful for them to sign an agreement, often referred to as a submission agreement (see appendices for examples), indicating their intent. Since any process involving arbitration means the parties are waiving significant legal rights, it is often helpful to encourage the parties to consult an attorney so they understand the scope of their commitment. The persons who set up such proceedings should also carefully explain, preferably in writing, the significance of submitting to arbitration.

The Christian Conciliation Service generally encourages the parties to use the med/arb process, which begins with substantial efforts through mediation. Should that fail, the parties automatically move into arbitration.

SELECTING THE MEDIATOR/ARBITRATOR   The parties must also decide who will act as the mediator(s) or arbitrator(s). The CCS maintains a list of lawyers and other Christian persons who have indicated a willingness to serve as mediators or arbitrators. In some CCS programs, teams of mediators or arbitrators (consisting of a lawyer, a pastor, and a business or professional person in the area of the dispute) are frequently used. Suggestions of those with particular skills or gifts that may be helpful in a given dispute may be made to the parties, but the decision is up to them. For instance, in a case involving a dispute over the disposition of farm property that was received by two relatives, the parties selected an arbitration team consisting of a pastor, a lawyer experienced in real estate, and a farmer.

What if the parties cannot agree on who will act as arbitrators? The Christian Conciliation Service has found very little difficulty here, but there are ways to resolve such disputes, which are common to other arbitration programs. Each party might select one arbitrator, then the two arbitrators pick a third. Or a list of potential arbitrators can be submitted to the parties, then the disputants take turns eliminating persons until the requisite number—usually three—remain.

DEFINING THE SCOPE OF THE DISPUTE   Since the legal power of the arbitrator derives from the consent of the parties, it is important that the parties clarify the legal issues that will be decided by the process. Undoubtedly other issues will surface, but it is still necessary to be sure the parties have agreed on the scope of the issues they are submitting to arbitration.

DETERMINING THE PARTIES   The fewer persons involved in a mediation process, the easier it is to move toward understanding, resolution, and reconciliation. However, it is important that all crucial parties are included, so the reconciliation reaches those deeply involved in the dispute. Often parties not legally involved may be the key to finding real healing (such as in-laws in a domestic dispute, spouses in business situations). No easy rule determines who should be involved.

PREPARING FOR A HEARING

Prior to the hearing, the disputing parties may wish to submit relevant documents; frequently each party prepares a statement of the issues as he sees it. A very special aspect of the preparation involves completing the "Readiness for Reconciliation" Bible study (see Chapter 11). This workbook/ study guide is designed to help the disputants examine their own commitments and spiritual lives so the Spirit of Christ can move into the conflict in a healing way. This self-assessment process is important to the whole healing enterprise.

Often the mediators or mediating team may meet with the parties individually before a formal hearing. While one must carefully avoid prejudging issues and short-circuiting the necessary direct confrontation, such preliminary sessions may help the mediators to understand the context of the dispute, the relevant parties, and their spiritual vitality.

THE MEDIATION SESSION OR HEARING

The exact nature of the hearing process will vary widely according to the nature of the dispute, the number of parties involved, the relationship of the parties, and the style of the team. Compared with legal processes, mediation sessions and arbitration hearings are often relatively brief, rarely involving more than one day. On occasion, a number of shorter sessions may be involved, with time in between to explore settlement options.

There are no legal requirements that govern the location of a hearing; any neutral site can be used. Many CCS sessions are held in churches to emphasize the spiritual base that underlies the entire process. Informal sessions with the parties are often held in homes to encourage a noncombative context.

ESTABLISHING THE CLIMATE   A central requirement for effective peacemaking in conciliation hearings is to establish the proper climate for effective communication and consideration of the whole range of issues. This climate must include a spirit of trust. The parties must feel that the conciliators are trustworthy and will keep confidences. They must see the team as open and neutral.

There must also be a sense of acceptance: a feeling that the conciliators are "with" and "for" all the parties. Spiritual concern must be a part of this climate. The parties must come to the process with an openness to the leading of the Spirit and a desire to see Jesus honored.

Finally, the climate must be one that fosters both listening and speaking. People should feel free to be honest, angry, open, confrontative. Each party will not only be allowed to speak directly, but will give the same privilege to others. This is a process of confrontation, but not a combative one.

The opening moments of the session are extremely important. They will include an introduction of the parties who are present and a summary of what will transpire: how the process will take place, its schedule, and its flow.

The conciliator should also clarify his role

as mediator or arbitrator. If a mediation process is involved, it may be particularly helpful to indicate that the role of the mediator is to facilitate the parties' agreement, not impose one on them.

Ground rules for the process should be discussed and agreed upon. One rule has already been mentioned: each party will have an opportunity to speak and neither will interrupt the other. The parties may need to be reminded of this rule during the session to keep their communication from becoming a continuous argument and battle for the floor.

ESTABLISHING THE SPIRITUAL DIMENSION   It is crucial to clarify the spiritual perspectives and commitments that have brought all the parties together. This will usually include some general statements: perhaps the reading of Scriptures such as 1 Corinthians 13 or other passages and a time of prayer. Of course the use of particular spiritual resources will depend on the receptivity of the parties.

In some situations, the mediators have found it helpful to begin by sharing the way in which the Lord has been real in their lives—meeting needs, providing strength, and giving peace and joy.

STORYTELLING   It is critical that the parties have an opportunity to tell their story, to get it all out. Each party should be encouraged to speak freely, recounting the facts, their feelings, their interpretation of events, and what they want to see happen.

We have often seen parties visibly express their relief and release when they have finished "getting it off their chest." So often what is at stake is not the alleged financial loss or "right," but a feeling that someone has taken advantage of them. They want an opportunity to tell their story.

The mediator may be tempted to cut this process short: to challenge perceptions or move quickly to some solution. But this storytelling must be carried to completion, unless feelings are so high that a cooling-off period is necessary.

During the storytelling stage, the mediator should listen carefully, communicating his attention nonverbally. Ron Kraybill of the Mennonite Conciliation Service in his book *Repairing the Breach* suggests that the mediator's primary role is to be a good listener. When the mediator speaks, it is as a clarifier. In particular Kraybill suggests that the mediator: "Listen for facts. . . . Listen for feelings. . . . Listen for specific demands. . . . Listen for offers of 'deals,' which may slip out without fanfare. . . . Probably the most important thing to listen for at this stage is why. Successful resolution will have to get to the root of problems and deal with underlying causes."

SEEKING RESOLUTION AND RECONCILIATION The storytelling stage should reveal the scope of the issues involved, the depth of the disputants' feelings, and their willingness to seek a resolution. The mediator may close this meeting by encouraging the parties to pray for wisdom and guidance.

After this session the mediator may wish to meet privately with each of the parties to further clarify issues and divide them into manageable units. Solutions, which may occur to the mediator, may be tested in a hypothetical way in such caucuses.

If the process is one of arbitration, the procedures may be somewhat more formal. In the labor and commercial area, arbitration is hardly distinguishable from normal judicial proceedings. However, in a Christian context this process should not neglect the spiritual elements and procedures that foster communication, openness, and sharing. In arbitration there may be witnesses, items of evidence, even cross-examination of witnesses. The parties may be represented by legal counsel. But the rules of evidence are informal enough to allow the parties to tell their story.

THE AGREEMENT OR AWARD

In mediation, the decision is an agreement reached by the parties themselves. This agreement should be written to clarify what the parties have agreed to do and to avoid vagueness and misunderstanding. Committing the agreement to writing also assists in clarifying its finality. Even signing it is a significant symbol. This written settlement is usually final, and the courts would normally enforce the agreement.

If the process is one of arbitration, the decision of the arbitrator(s) is referred to as an "award." The award may be announced at the meeting itself or subsequently. It is ultimately committed to writing. The award may also be enforced by court action.

PURSUING AND SOLIDIFYING RECONCILIATION
The role of the mediator/arbitrator may extend beyond the agreement or award into those aspects that foster total reconciliation. The conciliators may include a celebration of reconciliation or recommend some of the imaginative remedies suggested in this volume. But it is clear that the mere resolution of the dispute is not the full will of God nor of the conciliators. Christian conciliation involves a total reconciliation of the relationship between the parties involved.

10 BLESSED ARE THE PEACEMAKERS

It is the peacemakers, not the peace observers or celebrators, who are blessed in the Beatitudes: "Blessed are the peacemakers: for they shall be called the children of God" (Matt. 5:9). Anyone who has sought to mediate conflict knows that peacemaking is an exhausting and often painful ministry. It involves weeping with those who weep, just as much as rejoicing with those who have found resolution.

Peacemaking is a learned skill as well as a response to God's calling. It is also a gift and miracle. By its very character, making peace is also a work of love and art, a work of gentleness that is rarely praised. John Adams, a Methodist minister who was a mediator at Wounded Knee and a courier in the Iranian hostage crisis, observed that one can either make peace or get credit for peace—but not both.

Peacemaking is rarely mediating multi-million-dollar lawsuits. Nor is it necessarily being on the front lines of legal conflict as mediators or arbitrators. Peacemaking involves implementing these principles in our own personal relationships and churches as well as the more organized and systematic methods of the Christian Conciliation Service.

At times the peacemaker may be a prophet calling persons to biblical faithfulness in the midst of bitter litigation. Other persons may be peacemakers in intercession and prayer. All of us can commit ourselves to peacemaking in our own lives and neighborhoods: offering forgiveness and confession, being open and honest, valuing our relationships more than our rights.

This book has focused on the need for systematic and structural forms for legal peacemaking. We have hardly touched the international arena of the bitterness in Iran, Ireland, South Africa, and Southeast Asia. Nor have we spoken much of the social conflict in our own nation between black and white, Indian and Caucasian, political conservative and liberal. These are arenas, too, that cry out for peacemakers and reconcilers. The skills for peacemaking in international and social conflict will vary from the specific styles for dealing with legal and small group conflict. But the basic commitments and approaches are essentially the same because there are the same barriers to peace: hostility, alienation, lack of communication, labeling, and unforgiving spirits.

THE PEACEMAKER AS ENFORCER

We must not think of peacemaking as merely a passive or private role. It takes many forms: teaching, preaching, judgment, encouragement, intercession, and advocacy.

There are times when those who work for peace will demand that justice be implemented, agreements be kept, and integrity be maintained. This role is not really one of mediation or neutrality. The church may use its moral authority, and perhaps its disciplinary structures, to insist that its community accept biblical commands in dealing with disputes. Pastors are peacemakers when they urge disputants to apply biblical principles to their legal conflicts.

THE PEACEMAKER AS MEDIATOR

Mediation is not the application of formulas nor simply the skills of conflict management. It is a personal ministry, in which the commitments of the mediator are a central factor in the healing process. We shall look briefly at two components of the gifts of peacemaking: fundamental qualities of the mediator himself, and process qualities—skills and styles of mediation.

CREDIBILITY The most essential quality a peacemaker must possess is the ability to establish his credibility. Ron Kraybill fascinatingly refers to this as gaining a "passport"—gaining the credibility that allows one to enter into conflict as a mediator.

People generally learn through painful experiences that you can't really trust others. People will hurt you, break covenants, reveal secrets, and abuse confidences. So we all tend to guard against risking relationships, insights, and confidences. A central quality of any peacemaker/mediator is to break this cycle and establish credibility and trust, the essential "passport" Ron Kraybill spoke about. People who establish trust and credibility speak the same to all parties and guard the knowledge given them carefully. They do not ingratiate themselves to the parties involved nor do they use information to threaten, belittle, judge, or falsely praise the disputants. They are continually aware of the sacredness of the role they play.

The capacity to be a healer and reconciler is also clearly related to three other particular qualities.

▶113

SPIRITUAL VITALITY   In any ministry of conciliation built upon spiritual reality, the mediator's spiritual life is critical. Only one who
lives in communion with God, and nurtures
his own spirit in the Word and in community
with other Christians, can communicate the
presence of Jesus Christ to those in conflict.
The mediator is a priest in a New Testament
sense, stepping into conflict to bear witness
to Jesus Christ.

CARING   It is almost impossible to feign caring. Caring people are transparently loving.
They put others at ease. Caring people do
not press others into their agendas. If you
don't really care about people, then peacemaking is not for you.

VULNERABILITY   Peacemaking is not an abstract skill nor simply a managerial role.
Christian peacemakers may be called on to
share their own needs for forgiveness and
the alienation in their lives over which
Christ has triumphed.
   Peacemakers may find that before the parties can come to reconciliation they will lash
out in anger and frustration: the peacemakers may be caught in this cross fire and
absorb some of the hostilities of those in
conflict.
   Yet all of this vulnerability can be experienced as strength. Recognizing our helplessness may allow us to enter conflict as
reconcilers, knowing we must trust in
Christ's power. We will expect to experience
God's enablement in the midst of our own
frailty. We may, indeed, discover the truth
that God uses not the strong but the weak.
The best of healers are wounded healers,
persons who have wrestled like Jacob with
God and henceforth walk with a limp. Not a

few mediation sessions have begun with mediators acknowledging their uncertainty about how to proceed and their helplessness at devising solutions. They then suggest that only as Christ steps in will peace be given.

While the fundamental qualities of the mediator are crucial, there are also process skills that are necessary to effective mediation. Christian Conciliation Service training focuses heavily on developing these skills, but some of the qualities are basic.

COMFORT WITH CONFLICT Reconcilers must be persons who can function in the midst of strong feelings and alienation and not lose their own perspective. They must have the capacity to live with conflict and wait for the healing spirit to minister. Peacemakers must not rush too quickly to peace lest it be abortive, false, and not provide for a settled commitment.

AVAILABILITY Reconciliation not only takes work, it often takes time. The peacemaker must be one who is willing to invest energy and time. The qualities of care and credibility require patience, readiness, and openness, which expresses itself in availability. Those who wish to rush peace do not understand either the seriousness of conflict or the character of reconciliation. Ministries of reconciliation are frequently exhausting, not only in the actual time involved but the intensity of the encounters.

HUMANIZING An important skill in reconciliation ministries is the capacity to take conflict and humanize it. So often conflict is thought of in the context of justice, rights, and duties. There is a need to help individuals in conflict meet each other as persons, not mere collections of rights. Then they begin to see each other's feelings, hurts, hopes, and dreams. The humanizer can assist the parties in recognizing the commonalities of their experience and the values they share with each other. The humanizer helps people to shift at least a portion of the conflict from abstractions to persons. To use the terminology of the Jewish theologian Martin Buber, it moves the conflict from *I* versus *It,* to *I* versus *Thou.* And when I meet Thee, I begin perhaps to understand, to care, and to communicate.

COMMUNICATION SKILLS   While communication skills may at times be so overemphasized in secular conflict-resolution literature that they become almost a technique, communication is central to clarifying the issues and understanding the parties' concerns. In our own reconciliation in Christ, communication is central to God's process with us. The biblical words are, in fact, words of communication: Jesus Christ has become "the Word," which has been made flesh that we might behold it, hear it, and respond to it. God's prophetic call and the incarnation are his movement into relationship/communication with man so that man might hear his invitation to new life in Christ.

Persons in conflict often have truncated communication at best. They rarely truly behold each other. Their communications are distance-creating pronouncements that are often self-serving and argumentative. The legal process impedes real communication because it involves "third parties" and formalized structures.

The ministry of reconciliation requires the development of skills and the cultivation of styles that encourage open channels through which persons may meet. The skills related to communication are multiple, but among them are these critical capacities:

Listening Skills. The capacity to wait and hear—really hear—the concerns of persons: the pain and hurt, the hopes and dreams as well as the arguments and contentions. To allow persons to speak freely and fully and know they have been heard with empathy and sensitivity.

Questioning/Inquiring Skills. The capacity to gently and sensitively discover the unspoken concerns and to clarify ambiguities, not as an inquisitor but as one who seeks to understand.

Clarifying/Focusing Skills. The capacity to discover the central motifs and eliminate the peripheral, often disruptive, "noise" that precludes effective communication. The parties need to focus on the actual issues that lie behind their feelings and generalizations so they can see the real character of the issues that keep them at odds.

Information Resource. The capacity to act as a source of accurate information to prevent distortion and to expose rumor and innuendo. The effective mediator can provide information on resources, helpful parties, options, and remedies. This function will not be used in the early stages, but, as the parties begin to need accurate information, the mediator becomes a vital resource.

Confrontation Skills. The ability to confront others with the nature of their conduct and its implications for their own lives. Confrontation (which is often the first response of many who seek to be peacemakers) can be entered into too soon, before trust has been established. Then it actually inhibits healing and forces the parties into defensive postures. But once the trust relationship has been established, effective confrontation is often a key to helping parties choose the options that best express their ultimate commitments and faith. As David Augsburger suggests, care must precede confrontation and empathy must precede evaluation.

Resolution Skills. The capacity to assist parties in identifying the means to resolve the dispute and reconcile with one another. Such skills include helping the parties to evaluate the options before them in the light of their needs and values, encouraging positive movements, reinforcing solutions, and mobilizing support within their circle of friends for the positive steps that are being taken.

THE WEIGHTIER MATTERS OF THE LAW

Bill Gaither's song "The King Is Coming" anticipates the peace that will accompany Christ's kingdom: "In the courtroom, no debate." Hopefully it will be not only a pause in deliberations, but a whole new era, a redeemed way of perceiving and processing justice. There will be a different vision of the character and the process of justice. Then the weightier matters of the law (relationships and justice) will overwhelm the lighter matters of rights and property.

Though we sing this line about no debate, the debate still goes on. How striking it is that the author of that song is, at this writing, involved in a number of lawsuits against other Christian organizations.

We have a long way to go before that song may be sung with integrity and truthfulness. And it will not be easy, for it challenges so many of our cherished notions. An attorney who was recently advised to encourage his client (a Christian organization) to submit a dispute to conciliation queried, "Why?" He knew he would win in court, because his client was "right." It is hard to escape the presuppositions of our culture and our professions. No wonder Christ challenged us to new minds!

In Douglas Matthew's volume, *Sue the Bastards!,* there is an instructive section:

I'll trade away pounds of the cardinal virtues any day for an ounce or two of that vastly underestimated quality—spite. . . . Spite is a highly uncharitable form of anger that we are all supposed to repress because it's not very nice. The problem with that approach is that if you go around being nice all the time, the world's going to make a meatball out of you. . . . I don't think you are going to inherit the earth at all. . . . Better you should sue.

That probably expresses the options of the world's viewpoints. The Christian's ministry of reconciliation is, at its fundamental level, a totally different perspective on the character of this universe, on what is real and what is myth and illusion, on what is light and what is the product of the great deceiver. Being vulnerable, letting go, choosing relationships over rights may make one a sucker or a meatball from a secular viewpoint. But that may be the sort of death that rises with power, as Christ did, on the third day.

Establishing Christian options to the court system may be perceived as merely creating a socially more desirable option: unburdening an overloaded court, providing speedy and more humane structures, and saving excessive legal fees. Christian conciliation is all that. And it would probably be worth doing if that were all it was. But that is not all; that is not even the point. The central commitment is a profoundly biblical way of viewing our life together and our calling. It insists that we are a covenant people with a unique bonding under God.

Should the reader be interested in obtaining further information about the Christian Conciliation Service (CCS) or wish to make use of its national or local programs, he may write to:

WHERE TO GET HELP

Christian Legal Society
P.O. Box 2069
Oak Park, IL 60303
(312) 848-7735

The CCS maintains a number of local programs in major cities throughout the United States and, through its national membership, may be of assistance in almost any locale.

In addition to local conciliation programs, the CCS conducts regional training seminars on Christian principles used in mediation and arbitration, and publishes related materials.

11 READINESS FOR RECONCILIATION

Our experience has made it clear that perhaps the most significant factor in determining whether or not parties who do agree to seek mediation or arbitration through the Christian community are successful is whether or not they have been effectively prepared to confront one another in love and move toward reconciliation.

Merely throwing the disputants into the ring with each other and adding the presence of Christian mediators or arbitrators is not necessarily a healing process. The core of the concept of the church's ministry of healing of legal disputes is bringing the parties to the place where they not only understand the legal issues, but have examined their own lives and attitudes, have explored the relevance of central biblical teaching to their own life and to the dispute that they're in, and are fully prepared to meet their brother or sister or both for biblical confrontation and biblical reconciliation.

For that reason, extensive energy is put in by mediators and arbitrators working with the parties before any formal mediation or arbitration session.

A major tool utilized by Christian conciliators is a self study, *Readiness for Reconciliation.* This manual, available from the Christian Legal Society in a workbook format, guides the disputant through the application of a number of critical biblical themes. If used in a serious and disciplined way, it may not only be an instrument for inserting biblical principles into the dispute resolution process, but can be a means of enriching the disputants' own understanding of the Word of God in their lives—that is, it becomes a discipleship resource with an impact far beyond the present dispute. Here is an outline of that workbook and the issues which it addresses.

INVENTORY

Briefly summarize the conflict as you perceive it, placing events in chronological order as much as possible.

_____

_____

_____

_____

_____

Place a check by the following elements this conflict includes, cross out those it definitely does not include.

_____ Disagreements as to facts
_____ Disagreements as to the "rightness" or propriety of certain actions
_____ Disagreements as to the requirements of the civil or criminal law
_____ Disagreements as to biblical principles
_____ Personal feelings of hurt, anger, loss, or guilt

Write a brief comment in each space below indicating what effect this conflict is having on your life:

On your attitudes (e.g. resentment, bitterness)

_____

_____

On your emotional energies for your family and friends

_____

_____

On your personal devotional life

_____

_____

On your sense of joy and vitality

_____

_____

On your outlook in life (e.g. thankfulness, hopefulness)

_____

_____

On your finances

_____

_____

On your reputation in the community or church

_____

_____

This conflict could have been avoided or minimized if:

I had

_____

_____

The other party had

_____

_____

Which of the following feelings have you had during this conflict? (Check them.)

_____ Angry   _____ Proud
_____ Hurt   _____ Isolated
_____ Lonely   _____ Bitter
_____ Furious   _____ Guilty
_____ Thankful   _____ Wholesome
_____ Joyful   _____ Resentful
_____ Peaceful   _____ Sick
_____ Jealous   _____ Bouncy

How do you want to respond to this conflict? (Check your desired response.)

_____ Just settle   _____ Win
_____ Run   _____ Reconcile

Are you really ready for reconciliation? (Check those for which you are ready.)

_____ For honesty about problems and about feelings
_____ For openness about hurt and anger
_____ Readiness for forgiveness and love

What is the very best conclusion you can imagine to this conflict?

_____

_____

_____

_____

_____

STUDY 1
Reconciliation

I. Scriptures.

What is a prerequisite for worship? Matthew 5:23, 24.

_____

What is the task that we who have been reconciled through Christ have been given? 2 Corinthians 5:18.

_____

Describe Jesus' role as a peacemaker. Ephesians 2:11-22.

_____

II. Meditation.

How much was God willing to invest in breaking down the barriers so that man and God could be reconciled?

_____

How much was he willing to risk? To give?

_____

What does reconciliation mean?

_____

Is it just forgiveness, or absence of conflict?

_____

What is the goal of reconciliation?

_____

III. Complete these questions/exercises.

In the chart below, begin by writing your own definition of reconciliation, and then list 5 synonyms or words/phrases that describe what you believe *reconcile* means (e.g. "brought together"). Then list 5 antonyms, or opposites, of reconciliation.

Definition of Reconciliation:	
Synonyms 1. _____ 2. _____ 3. _____ 4. _____ 5. _____	Antonyms 1. _____ 2. _____ 3. _____ 4. _____ 5. _____

IV. Draw two symbols/pictures that reflect your feelings before and after reconciliation: on the left alienation, on the right reconciliation.

Alienation	Reconciliation

Imagine that the distance between the left and right of your symbols is 100 miles; that is, 100 miles represents the distance between total alienation and full reconciliation. How many miles do you think now exist between you and the one with whom you are in conflict?

_____

How far are you willing to travel?

_____

What would be a first step you could take toward reconciliation?

_____

_____

How would your relationship with the other person be different if you were reconciled?

_____

_____

Are you willing to put reconciliation ahead of winning?

_____

Name at least one person who has had a ministry of reconciliation with you in this conflict.

_____

Prayer: Lord Jesus, you gave your life to reconcile me to you, to bring me into your life and family. You suffered to win me as a friend. You died to win me as a child of God. Thank you, Lord, for breaking down the barriers and entering my life. Help me, Lord, in this conflict to really seek to be reconciled. Forgive my closedness and resentments. Open channels and doors. Destroy walls. Build bridges. Give me the capacity to want to restore and build a relationship of love and care. Through Jesus, the Reconciler. Amen.

I. Scriptures.

Psalm 133:1
John 17:11, 21-23
Ephesians 2:19-21

List four descriptive phrases from these texts which describe the believing community:

1. _____

2. _____

3. _____

4. _____

II. Meditation.

Why is the unity of the body of Christ so important to our Lord?

_____

What is it he is trying to create in his people that makes unity so central?

_____

If unity does not mean identity, but rather acknowledges differences and varieties of gifts, in what does the unity consist?

_____

How is it manifested?

_____

III. Complete these questions/exercises.

Are the parties to this conflict members of God's family, those he wants to dwell in unity?

_____

Name four things you have in common with
the other parties which can be emphasized
as elements of your unity.

1. _____

2. _____

3. _____

4. _____

Write your own version of 1 Corinthians 1:10.

_____

_____

_____

How can the way we deal with this conflict
demonstrate and enhance the unity of the
body?

_____

_____

How has the community of believers been
affected by this dispute? Has the unity increased or decreased?

_____

_____

What possible consequences of this dispute
could destroy our unity?

_____

_____

If you have had a history of relationship
with the other party, list two good memories
of those times—some positive moments.

_____

_____

_____

Rank these values on a scale of 1 to 8, giving 1 to the value with the highest biblical priority.

____ Financial success   ____ Unity
____ Vindication   ____ Justice
____ Clarifying "rights"   ____ Peace
____ Legality   ____ Forgiveness

Prayer: Lord Jesus, I know you are making a new people bound together in love and care. I know you are creating a family and both the one I am in conflict with and I are in that family. I don't sense unity now, but division and tension. Lord, bring us together, take our hands and press them toward each other. Help us to discover how very much we have in common. And may this unity help us to find a way to resolve this dispute that will build an even greater bond.

Memory Verses:

"Let the peace of God rule in your hearts, to the which also ye are called in one body" (Col. 3:15).

"We are members one of another" (Eph. 4:25).

I. Scriptures.

**STUDY 3
Sin and
Confession**

List under the headings below the teachings of these texts regarding our action, and God's action: 1 John 1:8, 9; Psalm 34:14, 18.

God's Action	Our Action
_____	_____
_____	_____
_____	_____

List what the Psalmist wants from God:
Psalm 51:1-17.

_____

_____

_____

List what the Psalmist says about himself:

_____

_____

_____

II. Meditation.

If sin is falling short of God's glory and his
will for our lives, then it probably infects our
lives even in ways we are not conscious of.
Sin consists not only in outright evil, but in
unwillingness to obey, refusals to grow, resistance to the promptings of the Spirit.

III. Complete these questions/exercises.

Make a quick list of 10 sins.

_____

_____

_____

Examine your list above. How many are
things you do? Place a + by them. How
many are attitudes? Circle them. How many
focus on relationships? Place a check by
them. Which are usually causes of conflict?
Which tend to be exacerbated by conflict?
Place an * by any which are related to this
conflict.

▶131

Has sin in your life contributed to the cause of this dispute? Name some specific short-comings.

_____

_____

_____

How has sin been a consequence of this dispute (e.g. attitudes, relationships)?

_____

_____

Is there an area of potential victory for you in your spiritual life, an area of growth which can be achieved through this conflict by confession and repentance?

_____

_____

Have you risked confession not only to God, but to your enemies and opponents?

☐ Yes

☐ No

Are there spiritual problems in your life now which keep God from really displaying his grace in this conflict?

☐ Yes

☐ No

Are you willing to open your life to grace?

☐ Yes

☐ No

Memory Verse:

"Let all bitterness and wrath and anger and clamor and slander be put away from you, with all malice" (Eph. 4:31, RSV).

Prayer: Dear Lord, I confess I am a sinner. My ego and pride get in the way of joy and life. My self-centeredness prevents the Spirit from flowing in my life. I focus on the faults of others. I expect others to change. Help me to be open to change. Help me to repent and be a new creation in Jesus. I release my pettiness, my securities, and my agenda to your care and will. Amen.

STUDY 4
Forgiveness

I. Scriptures.

Proverbs 24:17, 29
Matthew 5:7, 39-46
Matthew 18:21-35
Romans 12:14-21
Colossians 3:13
1 Peter 3:9

Look for attitudes a believer should have toward the wrongdoer. List 10 below:

1. _____

2. _____

3. _____

4. _____

5. _____

6. _____

7. _____

8. _____

9. _____

10. _____

II. Complete these questions/exercises.

Indicate 3 times in your life when others have forgiven you and accepted and loved you.

1. _____

   _____

2. _____

   _____

3. _____

   _____

What is the difference between forgiveness and mere avoidance?

_____

_____

List 4 antonyms (opposites) of forgiveness.

1. _____

2. _____

3. _____

4. _____

Which do you think is harder, to give forgiveness, or to receive forgiveness? Why?

_____

_____

In this dispute, what action of others could you choose to forgive?

_____

_____

In this dispute, what do you need forgiveness for?

_____

_____

Have you specifically asked forgiveness from anyone for your role in this dispute? If so, what was the response?

_____

_____

Should we ever ask forgiveness if we think we have done nothing wrong, but others believe we have and carry resentment? Does asking forgiveness imply guilt?

_____

_____

_____

Memory Verse:

"And be kind to one another, tenderhearted, forgiving one another, as God in Christ forgave you" (Eph. 4:32, RSV).

Prayer: Lord Jesus, thank you for setting me free by forgiving me. Lord, I have been hurt, I feel like a victim, and it's hard to forgive. It's hard for me to let go of my anger. I am hiding it inside me and storing it up. Lord, give me such a perception of your love for me, that I can truly give to others the freedom you have given me through forgiveness. And Lord, help me to accept the forgiveness others offer me, so that I may be released from guilt and be open to new joy with you and your children. Amen.

I. Scripture.

1 John 4:12-21
1 John 3:17, 18
1 Corinthians 13

What does each passage teach about the relationship of love to another believer?

1 John 4:12-21:

_____

_____

_____

1 John 3:17, 18:

_____

_____

_____

1 Corinthians 13:

_____

_____

_____

II. Complete these questions/exercises.

Write a paraphrase of 1 Corinthians 13:4-7.

_____

_____

_____

_____

Verse 7 refers to "bearing," "believing," "hoping," and "enduring all things." Under the four headings below, list a couple of things that Christ is calling you to bear, believe, hope for, and endure in this conflict.

Bearing _____

_____

Believing _____

_____

Hoping _____

_____

Enduring _____

_____

For each of the items in the column, give yourself a + for the items you are doing pretty well at. Circle two really difficult ones for you right now. Pray right now for God's strength in those two areas.

List three ways you may actively love some-one even if they don't love you.

1. _____

2. _____

3. _____

In which of the following ways are you man-ifesting God's will that you love the one with whom you are in conflict? Check them.

_____ Praying for them regularly and posi-tively.

_____ Thinking the best of them, not assum-ing the worst.

_____ Focusing on some loving action you can take, not on your feelings.

Memory Verse:

"And we know that all things work together for good to them that love God" (Rom. 8:28).

I. Scriptures.

Matthew 18:15-20
Ephesians 4:11-16

II. Complete these questions/exercises.

List the three steps Jesus outlines in Matthew 18:15ff.

1. _____

2. _____

3. _____

What reasons does Paul list in 1 Corinthians 6 for the church to be involved in disputes?

_____

_____

_____

What gifts and perspectives do you believe the church possesses that can be healing of conflict?

_____

_____

Name one person you know who is an effective peacemaker/healer.

_____

What persons in the church (fellow believers) have you consulted regarding this dispute? What suggestions have they made?

_____

_____

If you are willing to let the church fulfill the mandate of Matthew 18 and 1 Corinthians 6 and to abide by the decision, read and sign the covenant below:

Whereas I have committed my life to Jesus Christ, and myself to obey his teachings, and to find my peace and righteousness only in him; and whereas I have also committed my life to the church, his family of my brothers and sisters with whom I have oneness and fellowship; and whereas I believe he has called us to claim the gifts of wisdom and discernment in the body and to accept the counsel of our spiritual family, I am willing to follow the mandates of 1 Corinthians 6 and Matthew 18 and to abide by the decision of the church.

Date _____ Signed _____

Memory Verse:

"Brethren, if a man be overtaken in a fault, ye which are spiritual, restore such an one in the spirit of meekness; considering thyself, lest thou also be tempted" (Gal. 6:1).

STUDY 7
Peace

I. Scriptures.

Matthew 5:9
Romans 12:18
1 Thessalonians
James 3:17, 18

II. Complete these questions/exercises.

List in the diagram below five attributes/ qualities of a "peaceful" spiritual life, and five opposites of peace.

Peaceful	Not Peaceful

How can God give us peace in the midst of trial, temptation, and conflict? Suggest several ways.

_____

_____

_____

What actions on our part destroy peace?

_____

_____

Create a symbolic collage of peace, placing some symbol in each portion of the image below.

Draw a graph which represents the degree of peace vs. nonpeace in your life during the course of this conflict. Put some key words at the peaks and valleys to indicate the events which created these extremes.

Dispute Time Line

Peace	
Nonpeace	

What is something you can do, independent of what others do, to have internal peace?

_____

_____

What is one thing you can do to help create peace in this relationship?

_____

Memory Verse:

"Thou wilt keep him in perfect peace, whose mind is stayed on thee: because he trusteth in thee" (Isa. 26:3).

"Let the peace of Christ rule in your hearts, since as members of one body you were called to peace. And be thankful" (Col. 3:15, NIV).

In the light of the previous studies, answer the following questions:

The thing God wants me to learn from this conflict is:

_____

_____

This conflict offers an opportunity for:

_____

_____

The next step that God wants me to take in this dispute is:

_____

_____

_____

I will know Christ has been present in this situation if some of the following is evident/happens:

_____

_____

_____

To which of the following can you answer yes? Check them.

_____ I am prepared to lose if that means God will be honored.

_____ I can win without a spirit of victory and self-righteousness.

_____ I am open to the discovery that I am partly at fault.

_____ I am willing to risk forgiveness and confession.

_____ I am willing to risk a relationship.

_____ I can accept the decision of the church, even if I think it is wrong.

What Now—Ready for Reconciliation?

_____ I am praying daily for God's will to be done, not mine.

_____ I am ready to acknowledge my feelings and to confront the other party honestly with truth and love.

12 COMMON QUESTIONS AND ANSWERS

Included here are brief answers to some of the most frequently asked questions regarding the concept of Christian conciliation.

Does it work?

Probably this is the most common key "bottom line" question that we get asked. Certainly, even given a secular way of thinking about the question, the Lord has given us ample signs that when people apply biblical principles and biblical procedures to their legal disagreements, indeed a reconciliation *can* break through. At times, it even happens in miraculous fashion. There is a sense in which reconciliation in its fullest expression is indeed a miracle—a gift. It cannot be programmed, structured, or manipulated. What we can do is open ourselves to the working of the Holy Spirit, and certainly we've seen signs of that.

On the other hand, it is quite clear there is no magic in assembling Christians together in a room. Reconciliation is a difficult, often costly, and occasionally time-consuming process. The formal structures of mediation and arbitration may, in fact, only be occasions for small breakthroughs—first steps at genuine reconciliation. In that sense there often is disappointment in the degree to which people hang onto their disputes and resist reconciliation.

Also, of course, we must be careful in assessing what "works." We believe that following a biblically-faithful process is its own justification.

It is striking how successful the world has been at selling the notion that "religion" is about churches, liturgies, and doctrine and is only relevant for a narrow, constricted aspect of human experience. The biblical view of the lordship of Christ and the scope of the role of the church stands in sharp contrast with such a worldly perspective.

Isn't the church, when it gets involved in legal disputes, getting in over its head?

There is no area of our life which is not subject to spiritual principles. The church, as an instrument of God, an expression of his will for us to live in community and obedience with each other, touches every area of our life. It is only in modern times that legal disputes, issues of fraud or dishonesty, marriage and family relationships, have been perceived as beyond the scope of interest of the church. Church records up to the last century show that churches often intervened in such matters with teaching, rebuke, and discipline.

Sadly, the church today often is ill-equipped, both theologically and attitudinally, to be effective healers of legal conflict. The church itself, therefore, must be renewed and taught.

There are certainly some disputes in which technical expertise in law or some other field is appropriate, and the church may eagerly seek such skills as it functions as a peacemaker.

Basically, however, the church is not "in over its head," but being faithful to its high and sweeping calling.

What does it cost?

This question usually is directed to the issue of dollars, the "fee" for utilizing the Christian Conciliation Service or similar processes. In that sense, the fees are in most cases considerably less than the professional legal fees that would be involved in a civil lawsuit. Most programs associated with the Christian Conciliation Service charge minimal "filing fees" and depend largely on contributions for the operation of the basic program. Highly complex and prolonged efforts may appropriately entail additional fees.

Outside of the formal structures of the Christian Conciliation Service, fees, of course, may be decided by the parties involved.

It is quite clear to us, however, that there are other "costs" in this kind of process which may not emerge in secular proceedings—the spiritual and psychological costs of committing oneself to reconciliation, self-examination, confession, repentance, and restitution are not to be considered lightly. These may be free, but they are not cheap.

Is it legal?

As we have noted in other portions of this volume, the legal systems of every state provide by statute for arbitration of most types of disputes. Therefore, so long as arbitration efforts under procedures similar to those described here comply with the usually minimal provisions of these state statutes, the process is legal.

The general rule is, the decisions rendered by arbitrators are legally enforceable in the secular courts. Our experience has been that a properly conducted proceeding in which the parties have genuinely sought the Lord's guidance and have been open to the counsel of the church through the mediators results in a compliance which does not need the prod of the secular courts.

In the few instances in which decisions rendered under procedures similar to those outlined in this volume have been challenged in the courts, they have, with rare exception, been upheld consistent with the general principles of minimal judicial review of arbitration awards.

Are the decisions enforceable?

We believe that many of the basic principles outlined in this volume—such as principles of seeking peace, confession, and restitution—are applicable in all human relationships, including those among and with nonbelievers. There are certainly no scriptural warrants for treating unbelievers with a vindictive spirit. One ought to be as eager to make peace with the nonbeliever as with the believer. Biblical teachings about forgiveness were often delivered with special emphasis on forgiveness toward not only the unbeliever, but toward even the enemy.

Nevertheless, the special biblical admonitions of 1 Corinthians 6 and Matthew 18 are directed toward believers, and the authority of the church noted in many of these texts has its primary reference to the accountability of believers to one another and the church. With these principles in mind, so long as the parties understand the basic commitments of the Christian Conciliation Service in its effort to apply biblical principles, all disputants are welcome to utilize its

What about mediating or arbitrating with nonbelievers?

ministry. Some programs, however, while willing to mediate disputes involving nonbelievers, are reluctant to formally arbitrate under the principles of Matthew 18 such disputes since they do not have the same biblical authority for such decision making with nonbelievers.

Do you get involved in marital and other domestic disputes?

Few disputes today are as common or as tortuous as domestic disputes. The tragic consequences for families, children, and our society at large are evident to all of us. Our society, we believe, is paying a heavy price for the breaking of the marriage covenant.

The appropriateness of assisting persons in resolving child custody and other related matters involved in divorce is a controversial question. Local programs implementing principles of the Christian Conciliation Service have developed their own policies in this regard. A frequent policy is only to become involved in such cases with the approval of the church to which the parties belong, and with an understanding that it will be the commitment of the mediators/arbitrators to continue to work toward reconciliation. Failing that, however, they will assist the parties in resolving other issues in a less combative and hostile fashion. Often this emerges out of a deep concern for the children who are the unwitting victims of such battles.

What are your toughest cases?

The toughest cases probably are church disputes. It is tragic to admit that the place where biblical principles are the least likely to be enthusiastically endorsed is in the context of internal church disputes. Tragically, such disputes often have hardened the parties. They are likely to rigidly identify their own position with that of God. On principle they reject notions of compromise. They may even insist that their opponents are not even believers; therefore these biblical teachings do not apply.

It is sad that, in such context, the potential for a powerful witness to the community about a different way of dealing with disputes is lost. Even if a parting of the ways is appropriate, there are certainly more biblical ways of dealing with the usual issues of leadership and property than is evidenced in most church fights.

What are the biggest problems in implementing these principles and procedures?

There are a number of barriers that we experience, some of which are understandable and even legitimate; others are simply expressions of our disobedience or unfaithfulness. One legitimate issue is perhaps a lack of understanding of these processes and how they work. Though historically they have been employed in the church, we have lost much of that tradition. The processes sound new, novel, and odd.

Secondly, there is the issue of trust and credibility. Disputants are reluctant to release substantial monetary claims, or issues about which they feel deeply, to strangers using what they perceive to be an untested process.

Less justified is the resistance of parties to give up their "rights." They desire to continue in a "battle" mentality, to avoid direct dealing with the other party, and to value rights over relationships.

What if one party wants to use this process and the other doesn't?

This actually is the most common experience we have. One party is at least willing to explore the utilization of such procedures and the other party will not even consider it, either because of their own resistance or perhaps on the advice of legal counsel.

The key in such cases is to try multiple means of encouraging the reluctant party to at least examine the biblical teaching and familiarize themselves with the nature and character of this process. In this context local pastors, Christian organizations, and former disputants may be helpful in encouraging these reluctant parties at least to explore the options.

How does all of this relate to church discipline?

Historically, the ultimate sanction of the church was excommunication or—as it was called in other traditions—shunning, the ban, or avoidance. It was not uncommon in many periods of Christian history for the church to exercise such discipline whenever a member of its congregation went to court against another believer or in some other way violated the principles of Matthew 18.

We believe that there is a renewed interest in appropriate church discipline. Of course, simply administering church discipline in a judgmental way to persons who refuse to follow Matthew 18 may well be inappropriate, particularly in a church which has not structured its life and teaching in such a way that submitting to the body of Christ is a natural process. So we are convinced that the place the church must begin is with proper teaching.

We do believe, however, the church ought to use its teaching authority more, as well as the power of corrective discipline, to encourage and insist on a biblically-faithful

▶151

process for dealing with disputes among believers.

There is a tendency perhaps to see the procedures outlined herein as appropriate for the highly personal conflict kind of case, but to raise questions about its appropriateness in more complex litigation (such as those that involve substantial sums of money). The biblical teaching, however, does not seem to distinguish cases along these lines at all. There is authority seen for the church in all disputes among believers. There may, in fact, be certain technical questions which are appropriately taken before courts to interpret statutes, define rights and duties, etc. But the general principle ought not to be destroyed by such "exceptions."

It is clear that the amount of money at issue or the general complexity of the legal issues is not necessarily reflective of the relationship issues that may be involved. Some disputes, considered relatively minor from the standpoint of law, touch basic human attitudes deeply. People pursue lawsuits over sums of money far less than the cost of litigation. At issue in the biblical process, you recall, is not the mere resolution of the legal conflict but the reconciliation of the parties. Hence, new issues of attitude, spiritual maturity, and relationship emerge quite independent of the complexity of the legal issues.

For what kinds of disputes is Christian conciliation appropriate?

Doesn't this kind of process make resolving disputes even more complicated?

It certainly may. Principles of Christian conciliation do, in fact, often "raise the stakes." Not only are legal issues, parties, and remedies relevant, but we're likely to see a much larger range of questions, persons, and issues involved. Thus, what appears to be a minor dispute may, in terms of spiritual principles and reconciliation, be much more complicated. It is this dimension which both offers the most power to Christian conciliation and makes it the most threatening. It makes it no longer possible to hide behind legal issues or to hire persons to do your confronting.

Are these procedures confidential?

Certainly. One of the apparent advantages of Christian conciliation is an opportunity to avoid hanging out our dirty laundry. That's a strong consideration. Also, there is an element of privacy and confidentiality in such procedures that is important in encouraging honesty and directness, as well as confession and forgiveness.

From a legal standpoint, persons often wonder whether statements, offers of compromise, or admissions of responsibility made in the context of conciliation could be used later in court proceedings. Part of the answer is that the agreement by which people normally enter into Christian arbitration precludes subsequent court proceedings. However, if by lack of agreement or for some other reason subsequent judicial proceedings were instituted, matters raised in the context of mediation and arbitration proceedings would normally not be admissible. A rule of evidence precludes such matters which arise as part of "settlement conferences" from being put into evidence in court. However, these rules are by no means highly defined, and certainly statements made in such proceedings may indirectly provide "ammunition" in a subsequent war.

In another sense of confidentiality, while every effort is made to "contain" the dispute in keeping with Matthew 18—which sees initial stages as involving relatively few persons—Christian conciliation cannot make an absolute guarantee of confidentiality, since the last stage of the process outlined in Matthew 18 does involve the church. If we take the responsibility seriously, one may not privately persist in refusing to repent, or in being intransigent in regard to the counsel of the church, and hide behind a shield of confidentiality.

What is the role of the local church?

We have always insisted that the commitment to Christian conciliation, and the biblical procedures we have discussed here, is really the mission of the church in both its local and larger corporate expression. This is not a ministry just of Christian lawyers or of the Christian Legal Society, but rather something to which the church is called.

We have increasingly sensed that the effectiveness of conciliation ministries, both in a programmatic and individual case sense, is dependent on marshaling the resources of the church. These processes require the support—biblical and personal—of pastors, elders, and deacons. We frequently turn to local pastors for assistance in understanding and intervening in disputes, often asking such pastors to serve on mediation or arbitration panels.

The local church is vital in giving encouragement to parties to utilize such procedures. It is the church that provides other resources needed by disputants, sometimes providing for physical needs, but more often giving emotional and spiritual support and nurture.

Christian conciliation dare not become a "parachurch" ministry that is seen as competitive to the local church. Rather we are to be supportive resources for local churches, and collections of such churches, to effectively carry on this ministry.

What do I do if I have a dispute and want to use these processes?

The first thing, of course, is to apply the first step of Matthew 18, which is going to your brother in private. This is a vital step, and perhaps the most healing of all. It is striking how few persons involved in serious disputes have ever actually gone and spoken directly, one-on-one, to the other party. Secondly, one may implement these principles without the assistance of any formal structures either within a church or in a community through a program like CCS, but such structures may be helpful.

Local programs exist in many communities, and individual churches are increasingly accepting responsibility to assist in such processes. Contacting the national office of the Christian Conciliation Service, local churches, or local Christian Conciliation Service programs may be helpful in providing counsel and direction.

Who are the mediators or arbitrators that are utilized?

It is apparent that the spiritual sensitivities, gifts, and skills of mediators and arbitrators who seek to be peacemakers are crucial elements in enabling healthy conflict resolution. In a formal sense, the disputants agree on who the mediators/arbitrators will be. It is part of the character of this process that it's one of mutual consent. Often, of course, the disputants look to other persons such as the Christian Conciliation Service or local pastors or friends to assist in identifying persons with appropriate gifts and skills and the respect of the parties for any given dispute.

It is critical to identify persons who have spiritual maturity, who have healthy attitudes toward conflict, who can be strong resources, enablers, interpreters, and who have gifts of wisdom and discernment.

We have found, however, that by no means can one identify skilled peacemakers by professional degrees or certifications. Nor will skilled peacemakers alone be sufficient. The basic openness and attitude of the parties, and an imploring of the Holy Spirit to teach and instruct, are the real keys to resolving the conflict and opening the way to reconciliation.

Are there defined rules and procedures that govern arbitration hearings and mediation sessions?

A number of local Christian Conciliation Service programs have begun to develop the basic outlines of rules and procedures, but there is an appropriate reluctance to highly define the process. Too often such rules and procedures may become occasions for parties to seek to control the process or complain of its irregularity. Rules and procedures, if inflexible or arbitrary, may in fact impede the kind of directness and openness which is most critical to this process.

General procedures, which would be applicable in secular processes, are also often a major part of CCS procedures—e.g., the right to produce evidence and witnesses, to confront and challenge evidence and witnesses, the opportunity to be heard, etc.

In fact, one of the vital reasons why mediation/arbitration processes, even in a secular context, often are more successful than adversary proceedings is because there is a much clearer sense of participation by the parties. In a judicial proceeding, the disputants become mere observers who hardly understand the nature of the processes and are confronted with obscure legal language and technique. Often they cannot say what they want to say, cannot really confront other people, and are pushed into the background. This creates a sense of injustice.

In processes of mediation and arbitration, especially in the context of the Christian Conciliation Service, every effort is given to directly involve the parties. They have chosen to comply with the process; they participate in the selection of arbitrators or the means by which they are chosen; they have been involved in defining and clarifying the issues; they are encouraged to speak openly and freely; they, not attorneys and judges, are the key parties. Even persons who may feel they "lost the case" in a technical sense should nevertheless have a clear sense that they had been heard.

How does this process compare with secular mediation and arbitration?

In many important respects, Christian conciliation or arbitration is substantially different from secular or humanistic models of dispute resolution. Those differences are seen in several areas:

1) *Process*—An article in the ABA Journal entitled "Humanists as Mediators" (66 ABA Journal 576, May 1980), explained that the process of humanistic or secular mediation starts from this assumption: Given enough time, energy, creativity, good will, and effective communication, man—through his own intellect and effort—will eventually be able to solve his own problems and conflicts. There is perhaps even a distinct bias or prejudice against a Christian approach. As one director of a secular program stated, "The Bible is full of people trying to mediate conflicts. But most of those mediators were relatives or neighbors who had little to help

them but common sense." (Barbara Dodds Stanford, "Gentle Art of Settling Family Disputes," *Parade* magazine, September 14, 1980.)

The process of Christian conciliation is Christ-centered. It starts with the assumption that man, without Jesus Christ, will never be able to resolve and heal his own conflicts. Our own intellect often creates nothing more than compromise settlements in which the parties "split the difference" and go away not fully reconciled with their opponent. Jesus, serving as our Mediator, is really the central doctrine of the Christian faith.

As one attorney who has worked with CCS in a number of cases wrote, "It's my view that . . . the loser may come out feeling he didn't get rooked. The client might say, 'Okay, they conferred with us for twenty-five hours and they looked at the home and the kids and they talked it all over and everything else and, yet, I lost.' They're in a position where they might be able to make the best of a bad situation, which is what a custody case is, contested or otherwise."

As Christians, we believe that it is Jesus Christ who is the Mediator of legal disputes submitted to CCS. He is the one who creates true peace, healing, and reconciliation. We can only celebrate it; we are simply instruments of his peace. CCS is not merely Christian involvement in a secular program. Rather, it is a ministry built around a Christian world view, motivated by a commitment to follow the Lord's example as "our Mediator." As such, it brings into play some of the great and resounding themes of the Christian life.

2) *Mediators*—Christian conciliation believes that the mediator is much more than

a passive facilitator who helps the parties arrive at an agreement. The effective Christian mediator models his work after the mediation efforts of Jesus Christ in bringing about a reconciliation between man and God. For the Christian mediator to focus on Jesus is not a mere act of piety, but a serious intent to follow the example Jesus set for believers. Jesus not only taught a way to find reconciliation and peace, he demonstrated it. He *was* it. As John tells us, "The Word became flesh and dwelt among us." Thus, the Christian mediator follows an "active" rather than a "passive" model.

3) *Objectives*—The objective of the secular or humanistic mediator often is perceived as helping or facilitating the parties to arrive at "their own agreement." The mediator plays a fairly non-directive role. There is no "right" or "wrong" in terms of the character of the agreement or covenant between the parties that ultimately resolves the dispute. This is not true of Christian mediation.

The objective of Christian mediation is not just to facilitate reaching some agreement or settlement to which the parties will agree. It is, instead, to reach an agreement that reflects God's covenant will, which honors and glorifies his name. We have discovered that parties will sometimes, if left to their own devices in a non-directive mediation setting, arrive at settlements which a Christian mediator would not let them enter into as the basis for a covenant resolution.

For example, assume in one case that a teacher in a Christian school gives one of her students an F in English. Later in the day, the teacher discovers her car maliciously vandalized in the parking lot. She suspects the disgruntled student who denies any involvement. They come together in a mediation session and agree that if the student will pay for the car repair, his grade will be raised from an F to a B.

The Christian conciliator would not let the parties arrive at their agreement. The objective of CCS, through a process of *spiritual* and *factual* discernment, is to help the parties arrive at a resolution that is in accordance with biblical justice and God's covenant will.

4) *Causation*—A secular or humanistic view of the "causes" of conflict is generally much different from that view which the Christian takes. Secular analysis of conflict causation might relate to perceived incompatible goals or scarce rewards, the result of "personality problems," the interdependence of the parties, poor communication, etc. The Christian approach to the causation of legal conflict would treat these factors as important, but also as "symptoms of deeper root causes of the dispute."

The process of Christian conciliation involves discerning the levels of conflict. For example, there are surface problems such as visible actions of slander, dishonesty, argumentation, depression, or lack of trust. These are produced by "surface causes," such as guilt, rebellion, insecurity, and fear. Beneath these, however, are root problems that have to do with character—problems of bitterness (perhaps toward God); temporal values such as greed; and moral impurity or sinful thoughts and actions.

The root cause which must be dealt with in the process, however, is that of resisting the desire and the power which God gives us to live life in harmony with his principles. In doing this, we resist God's grace and violate basic scriptural principles of life. This root cause often deals with the nature and character of the disputants' relationships with Jesus Christ and, thus, is a spiritual problem which must be addressed as such in order to resolve the conflict and reconcile the relationship.

5) *Tools*—The tools of the secular or humanistic process of mediation or dispute resolution involve use of analytical ability, communication skills, empathetic understanding, restating position, securing compromises and concessions, etc. CCS does not ignore these basic tools. However, some of the tools of Christian conciliation along with those previously mentioned include prayer and intercession, liturgy and sacraments, searching the Scriptures, inner healing, deliverance, and many other spiritual tools. The work and ministry of the Holy Spirit and his gifts are vital to the work of the Christian conciliator.

Because the conviction that resolution and reconciliation take place in a spiritual realm is central to the CCS process, we view interpersonal and legal conflict as a part of the larger spiritual reality of this world. That is, we are not dealing merely with some human quarrel. The dispute is, in some sense, a part of the larger disunity of society; the alienation and separation that Jesus came to overcome through his church. Because of tools that invite the Spirit's presence, the mediators are always expecting the possibility of a "miracle" to resolve the seemingly impossible.

Other differences in *procedures* and *remedies* exist, as is noted in earlier chapters.

We believe there is a clear need for instruction and equipping, largely because of the lack of present involvement of churches, pastors, attorneys, and laypeople in applying these principles. The CCS has produced a variety of resources to assist pastors, churches and laypeople in applying these principles. These resources range from church curricula such as *Resolving Our Differences* (David C. Cook adult curriculum) to specific training conferences, offered in many cities, which try to enable people to understand the basic principles and to develop skills and approaches that make them effective peacemakers in both their personal lives and in formal programs.

How can pastors and lay persons become equipped to apply these principles in their own context?

In some senses, it seems to be. We have noticed enormous interest in the whole concept on the part of Christian attorneys and pastors. There is recognition that there is something fundamental here to the character of the church; something that could touch a deep problem and crisis in our society. We have here a ministry which is a healing, evangelistic, and pastoral ministry.

Is the idea catching on?

On the other hand, our experience is that this is by no means a matter of simply announcing a biblical truth and expecting persons to fall in line. We believe that when one starts advocating this approach there are indeed principalities and powers which resist it. Some of them are principalities and powers that exist in our general culture—our individualism, our materialism, our narcissism, our privatism. Others are in our own hearts—our greed, anger, resentment, refusal to submit, and resistance to forgiveness.

When one begins to touch these realities, it becomes clear that we are not talking simply about a new little church program, or a slight twist in religious activities. We're talking about changing an entire way in which people have viewed their responsibilities to one another, the degree to which spiritual principles would touch their entire lives—and that means spiritual warfare.

In fact, we believe that we are going to have serious problems of convincing disputants on an individual basis to utilize these seemingly radical and novel procedures until our whole mentality about spiritual life and the role of the church is so changed that one naturally recognizes the role of the Christian community as a healer of conflict. In other days, the culture of the Christian community was strong enough that it would have been almost inconceivable for people to have sued a brother or sister in the Lord, or to have believed that business or personal disputes with other believers were none of the church's business. Today, however, the presumption is the contrary, and it is that secular and unbiblical presumption against which the biblical principles that we've talked about here battle.

Why is avoiding the courts such a "big deal"?

At one level it might seem that resolving a legal dispute through the church isn't all that important. When you think of the resources that it takes, the investment of time and emotional energy to intervene in disputes, one is likely to happily let the court mess with it.

Two important factors, however, make such an approach tragic. First is the simple recognition of the broken relationships and alienation which so often mark the church today. No theme is more powerful in Scripture than that of reconciliation. The teaching about the oneness of the body of Christ, and the importance of the health of that body in its growth and mission, cannot be overexaggerated. We pay an enormous price for the brokenness, alienation, and insularity which are so much a part of life in the church today.

We believe the issue is even greater than that. We believe the capacity of the church to demonstrate a redeemed way of dealing with conflict is at issue. It is a sign and a witness to the world. We proudly profess that Jesus Christ is *the* Reconciler, the One who makes us new, who breaks down walls of hostility and makes each of us a new person, as is powerfully expressed in Ephesians. However, our convictions about the truth of the cosmos, about the power that comes into our lives from Jesus Christ, is likely to fall on deaf ears if we cannot provide a sample, an illustration, an incarnation of that power in our own communities.

If we cannot deal effectively with marital disputes, if business partnerships among believers become shattered and alienated relationships result, if we can't process the dissension and differences in our own church life and among our members, then how can we expect the world to believe that something new has broken in? We are not talking simply about reconciling Mary and Bill— we're talking about a sign of the power of Jesus Christ in the world. We are dealing with the highest of Christian proclamations about the character and work of God in the world.

APPENDICES

APPENDICES

1

THE UNIFORM ARBITRATION ACT

ACT RELATING TO ARBITRATION AND TO MAKE UNIFORM THE LAW WITH REFERENCE THERETO

SECTION 1. (Validity of Arbitration Agreement.) A written agreement to submit any existing controversy to arbitration or a provision in a written contract to submit to arbitration any controversy thereafter arising between the parties is valid, enforceable, and irrevocable, save upon such grounds as exist at law or in equity for the revocation of any contract. This act also applies to arbitration agreements between employers and employees or between their respective representatives (unless otherwise provided in the agreement).

SECTION 2. (Proceedings to Compel or Stay Arbitration.)

(a) On application of a party showing an agreement described in Section 1, and the opposing party's refusal to arbitrate, the court shall order the parties to proceed with arbitration, but if the opposing party denies the existence of the agreement to arbitrate, the court shall proceed summarily to the determination of the issue so raised and shall order arbitration if found for the moving party, otherwise, the application shall be denied.

(b) On application, the court may stay an arbitration proceeding commenced or threatened on a showing that there is no agreement to arbitrate. Such an issue, when in substantial and bona fide dispute, shall be forthwith and summarily tried and the stay ordered if found for the moving party. If found for the opposing party, the court shall order the parties to proceed to arbitration.

(c) If an issue referable to arbitration under the alleged agreement is involved in action or proceeding pending in a court having jurisdiction to hear applications under subdivision (a) of this Section, the application shall be made therein. Otherwise and subject to Section 18, the application may be made in any court of competent jurisdiction.

(d) Any action or proceeding involving an issue subject to arbitration shall be stayed if an order for arbitration or an application therefore has been made under this section or, if the issue is severable, the stay may be with respect thereto only. When the application is made in such action or proceeding, the order for arbitration shall include such stay.

(e) An order for arbitration shall not be refused on the ground that the claim in issue lacks merit or bona fides or because any fault or grounds for the claim sought to be arbitrated have not been shown.

SECTION 3. (Appointment of Arbitrators by Court.) If the arbitration agreement provides a method of appointment of arbitrators, this method shall be followed. In the absence thereof, or if the agreed method fails or for any reason cannot be followed, or when an arbitrator appointed fails or is unable to act and his successor has not been duly appointed, the court on application of a party shall appoint one or more arbitrators. An arbitrator so appointed has all the powers of one specifically named in the agreement.

SECTION 4. (Majority Action by Arbitrators.) The powers of the arbitrators may be exercised by a majority unless otherwise provided by the agreement or by this act.

SECTION 5. (Hearing.) Unless otherwise provided by the agreement:

(a) The arbitrators shall appoint a time and place for the hearing and cause notification to the parties to be served personally or by registered mail not less than five days before the hearing. Appearance at the hearing waives such notice. The arbitrators may adjourn the hearing from time to time as necessary and, on request of a party and for good cause or upon their own motion, may postpone the hearing to a time not later than the date fixed by the agreement for making the award unless the parties consent to a later date. The arbitrators may hear and determine the controversy upon the evidence produced notwithstanding the failure of a party duly notified to appear. The court on application may direct the arbitrators to proceed promptly with the hearing and determination of the controversy.

(b) The parties are entitled to be heard, to present evidence material to the controversy, and to cross-examine witnesses appearing at the hearing.

(c) The hearing shall be conducted by all the arbitrators, but a majority may determine any question and render a final award. If, during the course of the hearing, an arbitrator for any reason ceases to act, the remaining arbitrator or arbitrators appointed to act as neutrals may continue with the hearing and determination of the controversy.

SECTION 6. (Representation by Attorney.) A party has the right to be represented by an attorney at any proceeding or hearing under this act. A waiver thereof prior to the proceeding or hearing is ineffective.

SECTION 7. (Witnesses, Subpoenas, Depositions.)

(a) The arbitrators may issue (cause to be issued) subpoenas for the attendance of witnesses and for the production of books, records, documents, and other evidence, and shall have the power to administer oaths. Subpoenas so issued shall be served, and upon application to the court by a party or the arbitrators, enforced, in the manner provided by law for the service and enforcement of subpoenas in a civil action.

(b) On application of a party and for use as evidence, the arbitrators may permit a deposition to be taken, in the manner and upon the terms designated by the arbitrators, of a witness who cannot be subpoenaed or is unable to attend the hearing.

(c) All provisions of law compelling a person under subpoena to testify are applicable.

(d) Fees for attendance as a witness shall be the same as for a witness in the _____ Court.

SECTION 8. (Award.)

(a) The award shall be in writing and signed by the arbitrators joining in the award. The arbitrators shall deliver a copy to each party personally or by registered mail, or as provided in the agreement.

(b) An award shall be made within the time fixed therefore by the agreement or, if not so fixed, within such time as the court orders on application of a party. The parties may extend the time in writing either before or after the expiration thereof. A party waives the objection that an award was not made within the time required unless he notifies the arbitrators of his objection prior to the delivery of the award to him.

SECTION 9. (Change of Award by Arbitrators.) On application of a party or, if an application to the court is pending under Sections 11, 12 or 13, on submission to the arbitrators by the court under such conditions as the court may order, the arbitrators may modify or correct the award upon the grounds stated in paragraphs (1) and (3) of subdivison (a) of Section 13, or for the purpose of clarifying the award. The application shall be made within twenty days after delivery of the award to the applicant. Written notice thereof shall be given forthwith to the opposing party, stating he must serve his objections thereto, if any, within ten days from the notice. The award so modified or corrected is subject to the provisions of Sections 11, 12 and 13.

SECTION 10. (Fees and Expenses of Arbitration.) Unless otherwise provided in the agreement to arbitrate, the arbitrators' expenses and fees, together with other expenses, not including counsel fees, incurred in the conduct of the arbitration, shall be paid as provided in the award.

SECTION 11. (Confirmation of an Award.) Upon application of a party, the court shall confirm an award, unless within the time limits hereinafter imposed grounds are urged for vacating or modifying or correcting the award, in which case the court shall proceed as provided in Sections 12 and 13.

SECTION 12. (Vacating an Award.)

(a) Upon application of a party, the court shall vacate an award where:

(1) The award was procured by corruption, fraud, or other undue means;

(2) There was evident partiality by an arbitrator appointed as a neutral, or corruption in any of the arbitrators, or misconduct prejudicing the rights of any party;

(3) The arbitrators exceeded their powers;

(4) The arbitrators refused to postpone the hearing upon sufficient cause being shown therefore or refused to hear evidence material to the controversy or otherwise so conducted the hearing, contrary to the provisions of Section 5, as to prejudice substantially the rights of a party; or

(5) There was no arbitration agreement and the issue was not adversely determined in proceedings under Section 2 and the party did not participate in the arbitration hearing without raising the objection;

But the fact that the relief was such that it could not or would not be granted by a court of law or equity is not ground for vacating or refusing to confirm the award.

(b) An application under this Section shall be made within ninety days after delivery of a copy of the award to the applicant, except that, if predicated upon corruption, fraud, or other undue means, it shall be made within ninety days after such grounds are known or should have been known.

(c) In vacating the award on grounds other than stated in clause (5) of Subsection (a) the court may order a rehearing before new arbitrators chosen as provided in the agreement, or in the absence thereof, by the court in accordance with Section 3, or, if the award is vacated on grounds set forth in clauses (3) and (4) of Subsection (a) the court may order a rehearing before the arbitrators who made the award or their successors appointed in accordance with Section 3. The time within which the agreement requires the award to be made is applicable to the rehearing and commences from the date of the order.

(d) If the application to vacate is denied and no motion to modify or correct the award is pending, the court shall confirm the award.

SECTION 13. (Modification or Correction of Award.)

(a) Under application made within ninety days after delivery of a copy of the award to the applicant, the court shall modify or correct the award where:

(1) There was an evident miscalculation of figures or an evident mistake in the description of any person, thing, or property referred to in the award;

(2) The arbitrators have awarded upon a matter not submitted to them and the award may be corrected without affecting the merits of the decision upon the issues submitted; or

(3) The award is imperfect in a matter of form, not affecting the merits of the controversy.

(b) If the application is granted, the court shall modify and correct the award so as to effect its intent and shall confirm the award as so modified and corrected. Otherwise, the court shall confirm the award as made.

(c) An application to modify or correct an award may be joined in the alternative with an application to vacate the award.

SECTION 14. (Judgment or Decree on Award.) Upon the granting of an order confirming, modifying, or correcting an award, judgment or decree shall be entered in conformity therewith and be enforced as any other judgment or decree. Costs of the application and of the proceedings subsequent thereto, and disbursements, may be awarded by the court.

SECTION 15. (Judgment Roll, Docketing.)
(a) On entry of judgment or decree, the clerk shall prepare the judgment roll consisting, to the extent filed, of the following:
(1) The agreement and each written extension of the time within which to make the award;
(2) The award;
(3) A copy of the order confirming, modifying, or correcting the award; and
(4) A copy of the judgment or decree.
(b) The judgment or decree may be docketed as if rendered in an action.

SECTION 16. (Applications to Court.) Except as otherwise provided, an application to the court under this act shall be by motion and shall be heard in the manner and upon the notice provided by law or rule of court for the making and hearing of motions. Unless the parties have agreed otherwise, notice of an initial application for an order shall be served in the manner provided by law for the service of a summons in an action.

SECTION 17. (Court, Jurisdiction.) The term "court" means any court of competent jurisdiction of this State. The making of an agreement described in Section 1 providing for arbitration in this State confers jurisdiction on the court to enforce the agreement under this Act and to enter judgment on an award thereunder.

SECTION 18. (Venue.) An initial application shall be made to the court of the (county) in which the agreement provides the arbitration hearing shall be held or, if the hearing has been held, in the county in which it was held. Otherwise the application shall be made in the (county) where the adverse party resides or has a place of business or, if he has no residence or place of business in this State, to the court of any (county). All subsequent applications shall be made to the court hearing the initial application unless the court otherwise directs.

SECTION 19. (Appeals.)
   (a) An appeal may be taken from:
      (1) An order denying an application to compel arbitration made under Section 2;
      (2) An order granting an application to stay arbitration made under Section 2(b);
      (3) An order confirming or denying confirmation of an award;
      (4) An order modifying or correcting an award;
      (5) An order vacating an award without directing a rehearing; or
      (6) A judgment or decree entered pursuant to the provisions of this act.
   (b) The appeal shall be taken in the manner and to the same extent as from orders of judgments in a civil action.

SECTION 20. (Act Not Retroactive.) This act applies only to agreements made subsequent to the taking effect of this act.

SECTION 21. (Uniformity of Interpretation.) This act shall be so construed as to effectuate its general purpose to make uniform the law of those states which enact it.

SECTION 22. (Constitutionality.) If any provision of this act or the application thereof to any person or circumstances is held invalid, the invalidity shall not affect other provisions or applications of the act which can be given without the invalid provision or application, and to this end the provisions of this act are severable.

SECTION 23. (Short Title.) This act may be cited as the Uniform Arbitration Act.

SECTION 24. (Repeal.) All acts or parts of acts which are inconsistent with the provisions of this act are hereby repealed.

SECTION 25. (Time of Taking Effect.) This act shall take effect

2

MEDIATION AGREEMENT

_____ and

_____ are Christians, having received Jesus Christ as their personal Lord and Savior. Each person, with praise to God for the presence of the Holy Spirit in his life (Rom. 8:9) who convicts, helps, comforts, teaches, and gives wisdom, knows his love and unity in Christ for the other. Each party now earnestly desires to walk in a manner worthy of the Lord (Col. 1:10), with all humility and gentleness, with patience, showing forbearance to one another in love, and to be diligent to preserve the unity of the Spirit in the bond of peace (Eph. 4:2, 3).

Each person accepts the Holy Bible as the Word of God, and believes that it sets forth the principles by which God desires his children to live and be governed in their relationship with him, other believers, and nonbelievers.

The parties hereto desire to meet as members united in Christ's body, to resolve the dispute that has arisen between them regarding (here follows a statement of the issues in the dispute):

_____

_____

_____

_____

It is the desire of each party hereto that this dispute be resolved in accordance with the principles set forth in 1 Corinthians 6; Matthew 5:21-26; and Matthew 18:15-20. As between themselves, and in relation to the nonbelieving world, it is of paramount importance that the disagreement between them be resolved in a manner that honors and glorifies the Lord Jesus Christ, rather than that their personal motivations or interests be served. The unity we have in Christ is more important than "personal rights," and each party covenants to pray to be filled and led by the Holy Spirit as one relates to the other.

The parties agree that _____ shall act as mediator(s) to resolve the dispute between the parties according to the then governing procedures of the Christian Conciliation Service of the Christian Legal Society.

In witness hereof, the parties have signed this agreement this _____ day of _____, 19 ____.

_____

_____

Witness _____

_____

3

MEDIATION/ ARBITRATION AGREEMENT

SHORT FORM _____ and
_____ are Christians,
having received Jesus Christ as their personal Lord and Savior. Each person, with
praise to God for the presence of the Holy
Spirit in his life (Rom. 8:9) who convicts,
helps, comforts, teaches, and gives wisdom,
knows his love and unity in Christ for the
other. Each party now earnestly desires to
walk in a manner worthy of the Lord (Col.
1:10), with all humility and gentleness, with
patience, showing forbearance to one another in love, and to be diligent to preserve the
unity of the Spirit in the bond of peace (Eph.
4:2-3).

Each person accepts the Holy Bible as the
Word of God, and believes that it sets forth
the principles by which God desires his children to live and be governed in their relationship with him, other believers, and
nonbelievers.

The parties hereto desire to meet as members united in Christ's body, in humility

(Phil. 2), to resolve the dispute that has arisen between them regarding (here follows a statement of the issues in the dispute):

_____

_____

_____

_____

It is the desire of each party hereto that this dispute be resolved in accordance with the principles set forth in 1 Corinthians 6; Matthew 5:21-26; and Matthew 18:15-20. As between themselves, and in relation to the nonbelieving world, it is of paramount importance that the disagreement between them be resolved in a manner that honors and glorifies the Lord Jesus Christ, and not that their personal motivations or interests be served. The unity we have in Christ is more important than "personal rights," and each person covenants to pray and be filled and led by the Holy Spirit as one relates to the other.

The parties hereto agree that _____ _____ shall act as mediator/arbitrator(s) to resolve the dispute between the parties.

The parties hereto agree that the provisions for mediation/arbitration set forth in this agreement shall be the sole and exclusive remedy for resolving any controversy or claim between the parties. It is further agreed that each of the parties hereto waives whatever right he might have to maintain a lawsuit against the other party in a secular court of law upon the arising of such controversy or claim except as to enforce this agreement and any award granted through this process.

It is the intention of the parties that any controversy or claim between them shall be settled in a manner that is honoring and glorifying to the Lord Jesus Christ. Therefore, the mediation/arbitration shall first attempt to resolve the dispute through mediation. In the event that the controversy or claim between the parties cannot be settled by the parties, the controversy or claim shall be settled by arbitration in accordance with the then governing procedures of the Christian Conciliation Service of the Christian Legal Society then in effect. The decision rendered by the mediator/arbitrator(s) hereunder may be entered in any court having jurisdiction.

In witness hereof, the parties hereto execute this agreement this _____ day of _____, 19 _____.

_____

_____

LONG FORM   This agreement is made by and between _____ and _____ _____ who desire to meet as members united in the body of Christ (hereafter called the Christian Church) to resolve all of the issues in the following dispute:

_____

_____

_____

_____

_____

_____

_____

_____

_____

_____

_____

_____

CHRSTIAN COMMITMENT. Each party affirms that: they have received Jesus Christ as their personal Lord and Savior and are members of the Christian Church; they desire to be obedient to the will and Word of God in the resolution of dispute between them; they believe the Holy Bible is the inspired and infallible Word of God, governing all aspects of their life and relationships; the Scriptures give exclusive authority and responsibility to the Christian Church in any conflict between its members; they have been fully informed of the risks and benefits of alternative ways of resolving the dispute between them (including litigation, arbitration, negotiation, mediation, conciliation, and forgiveness); in spite of the risks, they desire this dispute be settled according to the mandate of 1 Corinthians 6:1-7, utilizing the procedure set forth in Matthew 18:15-20 and the substantive laws, Scriptural principles, standards of evidence and remedies of the Kingdom of God as set forth in the Holy Bible which is incorporated herein by reference; they are deliberately choosing to resolve this dispute within the Christian Church by reason of their shared conviction that it is better to be wronged or defrauded than to take a case into secular court against another believer as such courts are constitutionally prohibited from utilizing biblical procedures and law; the Lord will be present to guide these proceedings and speak his will to the parties through the peacemakers who will be called together in Jesus' name to resolve this conflict.

BIBLICAL MANDATE. Each party believes that: unity with other believers is more important than the exercise of personal rights or desires (Ephesians 4:1-6); they are never owners but always stewards of the property, money, and rights God Jehovah entrusts to them (1 Peter 4:10); they can trust God to meet their needs no matter what is given or forgiven in the course of this dispute; they have a responsibility to be peacemakers, healers, and reconcilers of conflict (1 Corinthians 5:18); reconciliation of conflict between Christians is more important than even worship (Matthew 5:23-24); no matter who is the primary wrongdoer, each party has an affirmative duty to initiate efforts at reconciliation (Matthew 18:15; Matthew 5:23-24); they should confess their sins to each other, repent, and pray for one another (James 5:16), even for one who wrongfully persecutes them (Matthew 5:44); they should bear one another's burdens (Galatians 6:11), forgive one another the way Christ forgives us (Ephesians 4:32), leave vengeance and repayment to God (Romans

12:19), overcome evil with acts of good (Romans 12:27), bless those who might revile against them (1 Corinthians 4:12), and love their enemies and their neighbors as themselves (Luke 6:27); they can trust God to meet their needs no matter what is given or forgiven in the course of this dispute; it is important to exercise patience, kindness, forbearance, gentleness, self-control, endurance, humility, and mercy and to be led by prayer, the Scriptures, and the Holy Spirit during the course of this dispute.

SELECTION OF PEACEMAKERS. The parties understand and agree that the Christian Church shall act through a panel of conciliators/mediators/arbitrators (hereafter called peacemakers) selected after the date of this agreement by the Christian Conciliation Service of New Mexico, Inc. (hereafter called CCS). The advice and recommendation of the parties and their pastors will be considered by CCS in selecting the panel of peacemakers. The individuals selected as peacemakers shall be deemed the "witnesses" referred to in Matthew 18:16. The parties fully understand and agree that these peacemakers may be selected by CCS because of a past, present, or special intimate relationship (either direct or indirect) to one or both of the parties.

PANEL MEMBERS. The parties understand that neither CCS, its staff, peacemakers, or moderators represent either party in any professional relationship, including (but not limited to) the attorney-client relationship. Comments, suggestions or recommendations by CCS, its staff, peacemakers, or moderators will not be understood to constitute legal advice such as might exist between a client and his attorney; nor will such comments, suggestions or recommendations be understood to constitute any other type of professional advice. The parties acknowledge having been clearly and fully advised that if there is a lawyer member of the panel, he represents neither party and they should not look to him to protect their individual interests or to keep confidences of one party from the other.

The parties acknowledge that, in a secular sense, there are risks of proceeding without separate legal counsel and they are willing to submit the dispute to the peacemaking panel in spite of these risks. The lawyer member of the panel, if any, may provide impartial legal advice and assist in reducing the parties' agreement to writing after he explains all pertinent considerations, alternatives, and consequences to each party of choosing the resolution agreed upon. The lawyer will only give legal advice to both parties in the presence of the other. The parties are hereby advised of the advantages of seeking independent legal counsel before executing any agreement drafted by the lawyer. The lawyer will not represent either of the parties in any subsequent legal proceeding relating to the controversy.

The parties further understand that they have the right to be assisted or represented by independent legal counsel in the mediation/arbitration process. The parties have been advised to seek the aid and advice of counsel with respect to legal rights which may be relinquished by the submission of this dispute to Christian conciliation or arbitration. In addition, the parties acknowledge that they have been advised to seek the aid of counsel prior to signing this agreement.

APPOINTMENT OF MODERATOR. CCS may appoint one or more moderators to attend some or all of the peacemaking sessions to help guide and structure the mediation or arbitration process. Such moderator(s) shall not be a voting member of the panel.

SCRIPTURAL PROCEDURE. The parties understand and agree that the basic procedure to be followed pursuant to this agreement is set forth in Matthew 18:15-20, as supplemented by any consistent rules of discipline and order adopted by the congregations or denominations of the respective parties, or any rules of procedure which may be adopted by CCS. Any objection to alleged procedural irregularities or defects must be raised at the time such occurs or is forever waived.

The peacemakers will first attempt to bring the parties into voluntary agreement through informal conciliation and mediation as set forth in Matthew 18:16. During this conciliation/mediation phase, the panel or moderator may make recommendations or suggestions concerning how the dispute might be satisfactorily resolved. The parties may be encouraged, but not required, to follow these recommendations or suggestions.

If the parties arrive at a voluntary agreement resolving all the issues in controversy, this agreement will be incorporated into a written covenant to be signed by the parties and witnessed by the peacemakers.

In the event the peacemakers determine that conciliation/mediation cannot bring complete agreement, any unresolved issues will automatically and after notice be deemed submitted to the same peacemaking panel for binding arbitration. During mediation or arbitration, the parties, their attorney, or the moderator may aid the peacemakers by appropriate questions, comments, suggestions of items, or proposed evidence. The propriety or admissibility of any question or proposed item of evidence will be determined solely by the peacemaking panel. During arbitration, the parties will observe the requirements of the Uniform Arbitration Act (Sec. 44-7-1 to 44-7-22, N.M.S.A. 19/8 Com.) except as otherwise set forth in this agreement. The arbitration/mediation proceedings will be conducted according to biblical procedures and principles with special emphasis on prayer, inner healing, the ministry and gifts of the Holy Spirit, scriptural counseling, confession and forgiveness, deliverance, biblical homework, and the intervention of the one true mediator, reconciler, and healer, Jesus Christ. After completion of the arbitration proceedings, the peacemakers will decide all of the issues in the dispute which were unresolved at the conciliation/mediation stage. Decisions may be made by majority vote. The parties agree to abide and perform any award or decision and that a judgment of any court having jurisdiction may be entered upon the award, findings, or decision.

RELATIONSHIP TO CHURCH LEADERSHIP.
It is understood by the parties that CCS does not generally become involved in the resolution of legal conflicts without the permission, delegation and participation of those in direct spiritual authority over the disputants: namely, parents, husbands, pastors, and church leaders. CCS does not purport to act as a pastor to the parties and recommends that they heed the following Scripture: "Obey your spiritual leaders and submit to their authority. They keep watch over you as men who must give an account" (Hebrews 13:17).

CONFIDENTIALITY AND PRIVILEGE.   The parties understand that CCS acting through its staff, peacemakers, and moderators may disclose other confidential information obtained by them to those in spiritual authority over the parties and hereby consent to such action.

The parties understand that the panel may seek to involve other Christian ministries in the peacemaking process and that general background information may be shared with them.

Christian mediation/arbitration is not a discovery device and shall not be used for discovery purposes. The information disclosed by the parties orally or in writing shall otherwise be confidential and shall not be used in any legal proceedings nor divulged by the peacemakers (except as outlined above) without the express written consent by both parties. The peacemakers shall not be asked nor subpoenaed by either party to testify at any hearing before any court or administrative hearing.

CHURCH DISCIPLINE. The parties further acknowledge that whatever is bound, decided, affirmed, or forgiven by the peacemakers will be confirmed in heaven and that the decision of the peacemakers is thus unappealable (Matthew 18:18-20). The parties promise that they will abide by the arbitration decision of the Christian Church as rendered by the peacemakers even though they may disagree with it. If a party refuses to abide by the decision of the Christian Church as announced by the peacemakers or attempts to appeal such decision in secular court the relevant scriptural facts may be reported to the leadership of each party's congregation pursuant to Matthew 18:16. It is understood that the denomination or congregation involved may proceed with discipline against the non-complying party or bring the matter to the attention of the Christian Church pursuant to Matthew 18:17. The party understands that disciplinary action conducted by a local denomination or congregation may be conveyed to other congregations or denominations.

The parties hereby agree that if they attend or are members of a given congregation or denomination at the time that this dispute arises or at the time of the signing of this agreement, or any time during the conciliation/arbitration process, that a cessation of such attendance or withdrawal of membership shall not preclude the church from proceeding with discipline as outlined above.

STAY OF ACTION.   The parties agree and stipulate that all proceedings in any pending legal action between them shall be stayed until the conclusion of mediation/arbitration process as herein provided.

ADDITIONAL INSTRUMENTS.   Each party shall, at any time and from time to time hereafter, execute and deliver any and all further instruments and assurances that the other may reasonably require for the purpose of giving full force and effect to the provision of this agreement.

AGREEMENT BINDING. This agreement shall be to the benefit of the Christian Church as a whole and shall be binding upon the parties hereto, their heirs, and personal representatives.

DEFAULT-BREACH.   The failure of either party to insist in any one or more instances upon the strict performances of any of the terms of this agreement by the other party, shall not be construed as a waiver or relinquishment of such term or terms for the future, and the same shall nevertheless continue in full force and effect.

SEVERABILITY.   Should any provision of this agreement for any reason be construed or declared to be invalid or unenforceable, such decision shall not affect the validity or enforceability of the remaining portion and the remaining portions of this agreement shall remain in force and effect as if this agreement had been executed without such invalid or unenforceable provisons.

WAIVER OF RIGHTS. The parties hereby jointly and severally acknowledge that they have had the opportunity to consult with independent legal counsel with regard to the legal and other effects of the provisions of this agreement, the rights and privileges granted hereunder, and all other matters pertaining hereto. Each party acknowledges his or her understanding that he or she is giving up and waiving rights which might well have great value under the secular law in exchange for the provisions of this covenant and each does so freely and willingly.

NO RIGHT TO WITHDRAW. The parties acknowledge and agree that they shall have no right to withdraw from the proceedings after an agreement to submit the dispute to CCS arbitration has been signed.

FEES, COSTS, AND EXPENSES. Each party agrees to pay to CCS an administrative fee of $50 upon execution of this agreement (unless waived by CCS). If the mediation stage lasts longer than 16 hours, then each party agrees to pay to CCS an additional administrative fee of $100. The parties understand that CCS may seek reimbursement for telephone bills, postage, photocopying, and any other expenses incurred in the peacemaking processing.

FUTURE DISPUTES. Should any dispute arise between the parties herein following the resolution of the issues and controversy specified herein, or should either of the parties have a complaint against the CCS, its board, staff, or peacemakers, such future disputes shall be submitted to a panel of

Christians for resolution and reconciliation pursuant to the terms and conditions contained in this agreement.

The parties acknowledge and affirm that they have read and understood this agreement and consent to be bound by all of its provisions.

Signed _____ Date _____

Signed _____ Date _____

Accepted _____ , on behalf of CCS

(This agreement is used by the Christian Conciliation Service of New Mexico.)

4

ARBITRATION AGREEMENT

The parties hereto consider themselves to be Christians. Each party accepts the Holy Bible as the Word of God, believing that it sets forth principles regarding the conduct God desires for the living of the Christian life in relation to God himself, other Christians, and nonbelievers.

Believing that God desires Christians to be reconciled to one another when disputes of any nature arise among them (Matthew 5:21-24; Matthew 18:15-20; Matthew 6:9-15), and desiring to honor and glorify the Lord Jesus Christ, the parties hereto agree that the provisions for arbitration set forth in this paragraph shall be the sole and exclusive remedy for resolving any controversy or claim between the parties arising out of or involving (here follows a statement of the issues in the dispute):

_____
_____
_____
_____

It is further agreed that each of the parties hereto waives whatever right he might have to maintain a lawsuit against the other party in a secular court of law upon the arising of such controversy or claim.

The parties hereto agree that _____
_____ shall act as arbitrator(s) to resolve the dispute. The process shall be in
accord with the then governing procedures
of the Christian Conciliation Service of the
Christian Legal Society.

The parties agree to be bound by the
above provisions this _____ day of

_____, 19___.

_____

_____

5 CONTRACT PROVISION FOR ARBITRATION OF DISPUTES

LONG FORM

The parties hereto consider themselves to be Christians. Each party accepts the Holy Bible as the Word of God, believing that the Scriptures set forth principles regarding the conduct God desires for the living of the Christian life in relation to God himself, other Christians, and nonbelievers.

Believing that God wants Christians to be reconciled to one another when disputes of any nature arise among them (Matthew 5:21-24; Matthew 18:15-20; Matthew 6:9-15), and desiring to honor and glorify the Lord Jesus Christ, the parties hereto agree that the provisions for arbitration set forth in this paragraph shall be the sole and exclusive remedy for resolving any controversy or claim between the parties arising out of or involving the Agreement. It is further agreed that each of the parties hereto waives whatever right he might have to maintain a lawsuit against the other party in a secular court of law upon the arising of such contro-

▶195

versy or claim except as to enforce this agreement and any award granted through this process.

It is the intention of the parties that any controversy or claim between themselves shall be settled in a manner that honors and glorifies the Lord Jesus Christ. Therefore, in the event that any controversy or claim between the parties arising out of, or involving, this Agreement cannot be settled by the parties, the controversy or claim shall be settled by arbitration in accordance with the principles found in the Bible with particular reference to 1 Corinthians 6:1-8. In the event that arbitration is necessary, each party shall, within fifteen (15) days after written notice is given by one party requesting arbitration under this paragraph, appoint one person committed to implementing biblical principles in the dispute. In the event that such persons appointed by the parties are not able to agree with regard to the settlement of any such controversy or claim within sixty (60) days from the date of the appointment of the last such person, then said persons shall jointly appoint a neutral third person and the three of them shall determine the controversy or claim. In the event the arbitrators cannot decide on a neutral third person, then the third arbitrator shall be selected by the Christian Legal Society under their then existing rules. The controversy or claim shall be settled by arbitration in accordance with the rules of the Christian Conciliation Service of the Christian Legal Society.

All decisions of the arbitrators shall be determined by majority vote. The decision rendered by the arbitrators hereunder may be entered in any court having jurisdiction.

The compensation to be paid to the arbitrators appointed under this paragraph, if any, and the responsibility for the payment thereof, shall be as determined by agreement of the parties. In the event the parties cannot agree, then a reasonable compensation shall be set by the arbitrators.

The parties agree to be bound by the above provision this _____ day of _____, 19_____.

_____

_____

SHORT FORM   In the event any controversy or claim arises out of or involving this contract/agreement, the parties, being Christian and persuaded that biblical principles mandate the resolution of such conflict with biblical procedures and principles, hereby agree that such disputes or issues which are not resolved by the parties shall, at the request of either party, be resolved by binding arbitration under the then controlling procedures of the Christian Conciliation Service of Oak Park, Illinois.

6

LITANY FOR RECONCILIATION

"All this is from God, who through Christ reconciled us to himself and gave us the ministry of reconciliation."

2 Corinthians 5:18 (RSV)

**ACT 1—
An Act of
Confession**

Leader: *"None is righteous, no, not one;
No one understands, no one seeks
  for God.
All have turned aside . . .
In their paths are ruin and misery,
And the way of peace they do not
  know."*
Romans 3:10-12, 16, 17 (RSV)

Leader: *"My grief is beyond healing,
My heart is sick within me. . . .
Is there no balm in Gilead?
Is there no physician there?"*
Jeremiah 8:18, 22 (RSV)

People: How clear is the anguish of our
  people.
The signs of our brokenness are
  all about us—broken spirits, broken hopes, broken promises,
  broken families, broken communities, broken nations.

Leader: We see it in courts.
            We see it in the streets.
            We see it in the schools.
            We see it in the churches.
            We see it in ourselves.

People: God, help us to weep, like Jere-
                miah, for the tragedy among us;
            Spirit of God, help us like Jesus, to
                weep over a city which resists
                its hope and calling;
            Lord Jesus, forgive us our personal
                and corporate sin
                which sets us against one
                    another,
                which builds walls rather than
                    paths,
                which nourishes suspicion,
                    then accusation, and finally
                    destruction.

Leader: Hear, O ye people, how even the
                rocks, the canyons, and the riv-
                ers yearn for the whole crea-
                tion's restoration to order and
                peace:

            *"For the creation waits with ea-
            ger longing for the revealing of the
            sons of God . . . because the crea-
            tion itself will be set free from its
            bondage to decay. . . . We know
            that the whole creation has been
            groaning in travail. . . ."*
                            Romans 8:19-22 (RSV)

Leader: Hear this demandingly simple
                word of the prophet:
            *"He has showed you, O man, what
            is good;
            And what does the Lord require of
            you*

**ACT II—
A Prayer for
the Creative
Word**

*But to do justice, and to love kind-
ness,
And to walk humbly with your
God?"*
Micah 6:8 (RSV)

Leader: And this word to 8th-century Israel, abundant in ceremony, but
impoverished of spirit:
*"Take away from me the noise of
your songs. . . .
But let justice roll down like
waters, and righteousness like an
everflowing stream."*
Amos 5:23, 24 (RSV)

People: How simple the words,
How easily they come to our lips:
justice, freedom, equity.
We are a people who delight in
words, who relish in the finely
turned phrase, the articulated
thesis—
The words flow. . . . They fill our
sermons, our courts, our legisla-
tures.

Leader: *God give them life.
God give them power.*

People: Allow those words to break with
new vigor in our communities,
churches, and courts.
May justice ring again with the
resonance of hope.
May freedom and justice again be
the commerce of our natural life.

Creative God, whose words create, whose concepts liberate,
and whose WORD became incar-
nate—

Give your life and spirit to our
words.
Let us use them sparingly but
powerfully,
Cautiously but hopefully.

**ACT III—
An Openness
to
Servanthood**

Leader: *"Have this mind among yourselves,
which is yours in Christ Jesus,
Who, though he was in the form of
God,
Did not count equality with God a
thing to be grasped,
But emptied himself, taking the
form of a servant. . . ."*
Philippians 2:5-7 (RSV)

Leader: *"All this is from God, who through
Christ reconciled us to himself
and gave us the ministry of reconciliation."*
2 Corinthians 5:18 (RSV)

People: Lord God, servanthood is not easy
for us.
We are attracted to the illusions of
power and rank.
We are seduced by wealth and
privilege.
We are accustomed to success and
surrounded by the symbols of
our accomplishments.
The towel and basin of servanthood,
The stooping of ministry,
The listening, gentleness, and
openness of the serving spirit
are so alien to much of our society—and to us.

O God, who ministers to us,
Who breaks open the storehouse

of treasures before us,
who came to the sick,
   not the well,
who touched the leper, forgave
   the harlot, endorsed the Sa-
   maritan, welcomed the child,
   dined with the tax collector,
   and was numbered with the
   sinners,

Leader: *Teach us to love.*
Teach us to serve.
Teach us gentle strength and
   warm authority.
Teach us how to bind up the bro-
   kenness.
Teach us to be stewards of our
   powers, custodians of our com-
   munities.
Teach us the sheer, exploding joy
   of service.

People: Let us be living witnesses of reconciliation, harmony, forgive-
ness, understanding, and
brotherhood.
Drive out of us and those with
whom we deal, those contentious spirits, those unyielding attitudes of false superiority, those
divisions and hostilities in our
own professions which sap the
vitality of our corporate calling.

**ACT IV—
A Plea for
Peace**

Leader: *"And his name will be called*
Wonderful Counselor, Mighty God,
Everlasting Father, Prince of
   Peace."

Isaiah 9:6 (RSV)

▶203

Leader: *"For he is our peace, who has made us both one, and has broken down the dividing wall of hostility. . . .*
And he came and preached peace to you who were far off and peace to those who were near."
Ephesians 2:14, 17 (RSV)

Leader: In the hostility of conflict and the bitterness of dispute—

People: Grant that we may work for peace.

Leader: In the courts and churches alike,

People: Grant, O God, that we may speak for peace.

Leader: In the communities, the cities, and the country,

People: Grant, O Lord, that we may be lovers of peace.

Leader: In the raging tensions and social turmoil of our day,

People: Grant, O Christ, that we may be sowers of seeds of peace, waterers of those others have planted, and harvesters of those now grown and mature.

Leader: And this very day, O God, give us the courage, the vision, and the will to seek for signs of the kingdom where peace reigns, where swords and spears become plows and pruning hooks.

People: Let us indeed see the kingdom.
Let us anticipate the miracle of
   peace,
   the joy of reconciliation,
   the celebration of understand-
     ing,
   the glory of justice, and
   the triumph of love.

ST. FRANCIS'S PRAYER

Lord, make me an instrument of Thy peace.
Where there is hate, may I bring love;
Where offense, may I bring pardon;
May I bring union in place of discord;
Truth, replacing error;
Faith, where once there was doubt;
Hope, for despair;
Light, where was darkness;
Joy to replace sadness.
Make me not to so crave to be loved as to
   love.
Help me to learn that in giving I may re-
   ceive;
In forgetting self, I may find life eternal.

St. Francis of Assisi, 1182-1226

Prepared by Lynn
R. Buzzard, Execu-
tive Director.

NOTES

INTRODUCTION

1. Karen B. Mains, *The Key to a Loving Heart* (Elgin, Ill.: David C. Cook Pub. Co., 1979), pp. 143-44.

CHAPTER 2

1. Jerold Auerbach, "Plague of Lawyers," *Harpers* (October 1976), p. 38.

CHAPTER 4

1. Samuel Ericsson, "How to Avoid a Lawsuit," *Christian Life* (May 1981), pp. 27, 47, 48.

CHAPTER 8

1. Jerome W. Wright, "The Church As an Agent for Dispute Settlement: A Bahamian Out-Island Example," *Journal of Religious Thought* 35, no. 1 (1978): 27.
2. Menachem Elon, "The Source and Nature of Jewish Law and Its Application in the State of Israel," *Israel Law Review* 2, no. 4 (1967): 517.
3. Ibid., pp. 520-21.

ANNOTATED BIBLIOGRAPHY

I. Resources related to the Christian Conciliation Service.

Agents of Reconciliation. Christian Conciliation Service.
A collection of Scripture verses on separate cards in a vinyl packet. Each verse deals with an aspect of the biblical invitation to reconciliation, peacemaking, justice, unity, and redemptive surrender.

Buzzard, Lynn R., and Kraybill, Ron. *Mediation/Arbitration: A Reader.* Oak Park: Christian Legal Society, and Akron: Mennonite Central Committee, 1980. Revised 1982.
A collection of articles and essays on conflict mediation including an extensive bibliography. Aimed at Christians, it outlines the biblical and ethical dimensions of conciliation.

Buzzard, Lynn and Juanita, and Eck, Laury *Readiness for Reconciliation.* Oak Park: Christian Legal Society, 1982.
A biblical guide designed to assist persons in assessing their readiness for reconciliation in the midst of conflicts and disputes.

Buzzard, Lynn and Juanita. *Resolving Our Differences.* Elgin: David C. Cook Publishing Co., 1982.

A multimedia teaching kit designed for use in small groups, includes plans and resources (handouts, overhead transparencies, duplicate masters, etc.) to introduce persons to the biblical teachings concerning reconciliation.

Pahlen-Fedoroff, Gerald von. *Biblical Conflict Resolution.* Oak Park: Christian Legal Society, 1982.

A survey and explication of biblical texts related to major aspects of conflict resolution such as: forgiveness, restitution, conflicts among believers and unbelievers, and conflicts with the state.

The Reconciler. Christian Legal Society.

A publication of the Christian Conciliation Service that contains news stories regarding CCS, case reports on issues handled, and suggested resources and articles related to Christian conciliation practice and theology.

Wilson, John F. *Relationships.* Carol Stream: Hope Publishing Co., 1982.

A musical of the ministry of reconciliation, commissioned by CLS for presentation at its first national CCS conference. Scores, stereo records/cassettes, and instrumental tapes/cassettes available.

II. Other Publications

THE ADVERSARY SYSTEM

Many recent books challenge the adequacy of our adversary legal system to resolve disputes and reconcile the parties to the disputes.

Alper, Benedict S., and Nichols, Lawrence T. *Beyond the Courtroom.* Lexington: D.C. Heath & Co., Lexington Books, 1981.

Surveys new community modes of justice (other than the adversary system) that have their foundation in healing, reconciliation, and restitution. Concentrating primarily on new programs in criminal justice, it focuses on issues such as assistance and compensation to victims, arbitration and mediation, and a variety of informal and community court models in the U.S. and other countries.

Marks, Marlene Adler, *The Suing of America.* New York: Seaview Books, 1981.
Why and how we take each other to court in this country. This book would be useful to the legal peacemaker in understanding why Americans fight and complain in the courtroom.

Strick, Anne. *Injustice for All: How Our Adversary System of Law Victimizes Us and Subverts Justice.* New York: G. P. Putnam's Sons, 1977.
A powerful indictment of the legal adversary system in the U.S. Although not written from a Christian viewpoint, the book provides evidence for a new approach to legal conflict based on biblical principles.

CHRISTIAN CONFLICT RESOLUTION
The following materials deal very specifically with the reconciliation of legal and community disputes from a Christian perspective.

Adams, John P. *At the Heart of the Whirlwind.* New York: Harper & Row Pubs., 1976.
A close-up view of nationally known conflicts by a Methodist minister who was there as a mediator. The author lays back the cover of controversies such as Martin Luther King's assassination, Kent State, Wounded Knee, and the 1971 Miami Beach political convention. He tells what strategies went into the resolution of the conflicts.

Fairfield, James G. T. *When You Don't Agree.* Scottsdale: Herald Press, 1977.
A manual on how to handle conflicts without straining relationships—while hopefully achieving personal growth. This text would be useful as a training manual for any mediator or arbitrator. Included are chapters on common conflict skills, confronting the problem, and setting new conflict patterns.

Howe, Reuel. *The Miracle of Dialogue.* New York: Seabury Press, 1963.
Discusses and analyzes dialogue as an essential ingredient in all conflict resolution. The author sees it as the principle of effective communication between the parties in dispute. As he concludes, "The fruit of dialogue is the reunion of man with himself, with others, and with God."

Kraybill, Ron. *Repairing the Breach: Ministering in Community Conflict.* Akron: Mennonite Central Committee, 1980.
A concise book designed to help the peacemaker explain, in concrete terms, what he or she aims to do so that the confidence of the parties will not be lost before the task is done. It is an attempt, using actual cases and illustrations of the Mennonite Conciliation Service, to bring conflict resolution within the realm of the possible for nonexperts.

Carlson, Dwight L. *Overcoming Hurts and Anger.* Irvine: Harvest House Pubs., 1981.
Notes how to identify and cope with the negative emotions that often surface during the course of a legal dispute. This book would help the peacemaker identify and cope with the feelings of hurt and anger that are being experienced by the parties in the conflict.

Scanzoni, John. *Love and Negotiate: Creative*

Conflict in Marriage. Waco: Word Books, 1979.
Presents some unique insights into behavior patterns that cause conflict. The author suggests new ways of resolving conflict, such as mutual submission. He examines the use and abuse of power in conflict resolution. Chapters deal with female-male conflict, the biblical basis for conflict and negotiation, approaching marital conflict, building marital accords, living with disagreement, and avoiding deadlocks and stagnation. Some might question the scriptural foundation of this book.

Schaeffer, Edith. *Affliction.* Old Tappan: Fleming H. Revell, 1978.
Deals comprehensively with a Christian understanding of the reality of pain and suffering in our lives—which often comes in the form of serious conflict with others. This book points up the many possible biblical sources of human suffering and explores ways in which those being "afflicted" can find answers for themselves.

Simundsom, Daniel J. *Faith Under Fire: Biblical Interpretations of Suffering.* Minneapolis: Augsburg Publishing House, 1980.
Suggests fresh ways for the resources of Scripture to be used during the times of crisis represented by legal conflict. The book discusses the basic biblical view of suffering, suffering for others, Job and the Counselors, and how to give comfort and hope to those who are suffering.

Sumrall, Lester. *Hostility.* New York: Thomas Nelson, 1981.
Approaches hostility from a Christian perspective that, paradoxically, views the world's growing hostility and conflict with anticipation and hope. From this text, the

Christian peacemaker can learn how to deal in a biblical manner with potentially destructive emotions arising during a dispute. Covers subjects such as the causes and effects of hostility, the mind and hostility, do-it-yourself kits, what Jesus said and did about hostility, hostility and the end times, and how to destroy hostility.

CHRISTIAN HEALING

Many materials in the area of Christian healing—physical, emotional, and spiritual—are applicable to the healing of relationships which are often fractured in the course of conflict.

Scalan, Michael. *The Power in Penance.* Notre Dame: Ave Maria Press, 1972. Deals with the role of confession and the Holy Spirit in the healing process. The author, who is a Franciscan with a Juris Doctorate from Harvard, shows how to use the power in the sacrament of penance in reconciling relationships.

Stedman, Ray C. *Spiritual Warfare.* Waco: Word Books, 1975. Recognizes that behind legal disputes between Christians lies the craft and power of the great spiritual being that Jesus called the ruler of this world. The author sees conflicts as a spiritual battle and maps out a strategy the peacemaker can use for combating the Devil's evil forces.

COUNSELING

Collins, Gary. *How to Be a People Helper.* Santa Ana: Vision House Publishers, 1976. Designed to help the reader become a better people helper, sensitive to the feelings, needs, and pains of people. This book helps the peacemaker learn to deal with "people-problem" crises and learn how to use the same principles that are used by professionals in helping people and to know when a referral is necessary.

Wakefield, Norman. *Listening, A Christian's Guide to Loving Relationships.* Waco: Word Books, 1981.

Demonstrates the hows and whys of effective listening. The book would help the conciliator improve his listening skills, help build stronger relationships, and overcome listening barriers and bad listening habits.

FORGIVENESS

Augsburger, David. *Caring Enough to Forgive.* Glendale: Regal Books, 1981.

Discusses and analyzes the differences between true and false forgiveness in more depth than any other source. The issue of forgiveness is one that arises in any legal dispute between Christians. Highly recommended to the peacemaker.

Justice, William G. *Guilt and Forgiveness.* Grand Rapids: Baker Book House, 1980.

Provides a biblically based solution for anyone struggling with a sense of guilt. The author, writing in the manner of courtroom drama, shows the natural destructiveness of sin and man's need for atonement and reconciliation.

Lockerbie, Jeanette. *Forgive, Forget and Be Free.* Chappaqua: Christian Herald Books, 1981.

Demonstrates how the Christian, in the midst of legal conflict, can sever the chains of bitterness, hatred, anger, greed, and remorse. It illustrates concrete, scripturally based ways to "bury the hatchet" and achieve inner release from the torment of an unforgiving spirit. Issues that make forgiveness difficult or seemingly impossible are dealt with in a manner useful to the peacemaker.

MANAGING CONFLICT WITHIN THE CHURCH

Principles of managing conflict within a local church are generally applicable to the resolution of disputes between Christians of different denominations.

Chandler, Walter M. *The Trial of Jesus.* Norcross: Harrison Co., 1956.

An exhaustive treatise on the trials of Jesus. It is useful to the peacemaker in that it clearly demonstrates the rights which Jesus laid down and the pains suffered that we might be reconciled to God the Father.

Flynn, Leslie B. *Great Church Fights.* Wheaton: Victor Books, 1977.

Verifies that the problems causing legal disputes and divisions today are not different from those in the New Testament churches. Many of the New Testament controversies are interpreted and peacemakers are shown, in the spirit of love, how to face problems of conflict between church members today.

Leas, Speed. *A Lay Person's Guide to Conflict Management.* Washington, D.C.: Alban Institute, 1979.

A short booklet written for those who find conflict within their congregations and want to resolve it. Included are sections on what people fight about, why people fight, what people do that is not helpful when they fight in the church, what attitudes are helpful in managing conflict, what the goals are of the conflict management process, and what the individual can do to manage conflict.

Leas, Speed, and Kittlaus, Paul. *Church Fights: Managing Conflict in the Local Church.* Philadelphia: Westminster Press, 1977.
A manual for those who want to resolve conflict in their church. It does not deal theoretically with the subject of conflict management, nor does it contain many biblical references. Rather it analyzes assumptions and preconceptions about conflict, then covers how to begin managing a dispute, conflict management without a referee, determining what information is necessary to resolve a dispute, and strategies of interpersonal conflict resolution.

Miller, John M. *The Contentious Community: Constructive Conflict in the Church.* Philadelphia: Westminster Press, 1978.
A well-written book on how to constructively cope with conflict in the church. The author examines some of the tensions that cause conflict between Christians. He argues that the church is called on to serve as a peacemaker and to create unity and reconciliation in the midst of its natural diversity. Includes a provocative set of discussion questions on conflict and the church.

PEACEMAKING
Literature dealing with the general area of Christian peacemaking is applicable to interpersonal and legal conflict.

Arnett, Ronald C. *Dwell in Peace.* Elgin: Brethren Press, 1980.
A valuable biblical perspective on how to handle conflict and eliminate violence in relationships. This is a book about interpersonal communication that can help the conciliator apply principles of reconciliation, nonviolence, and caring dialogue to

conflicts in the home, on the job, or in the
neighborhood.

Eller, Vernard. *War and Peace from Genesis
to Revelation.* Scottsdale: Herald Press,
1981.
Deals not only with war but interpersonal
conflict throughout the Scriptures.

Shelly, Maynard. *New Call for Peacemakers.*
Newton: Faith and Life Press, 1979.
Calls for justice and peace, evangelism
and peacemaking, nonresistance and
overcoming evil with good, service and
prophecy, personal and political witness.
The author places the peacemaking ministry within the framework of a biblical and
Spirit-led faith.